Economic Atlas of the Soviet Union

By George Kish

With the assistance of

IAN M. MATLEY, *Research Associate*

HOLLY FRY, *Research Assistant*

and **BETTY BELLAIRE,** *Cartographer*

Economic Atlas of the Soviet Union

SECOND EDITION, REVISED

Ann Arbor **The University of Michigan Press**

Contents

Introduction

The emergence of the Soviet Union as a world industrial power of the first magnitude is one of the most significant events of the second half of the twentieth century. This atlas portrays the spatial distribution of the principal elements of the Soviet economy.

We present a series of cartographic portraits of the Soviet economy, showing the present status of farming, mining, industry, transportation, and urbanization. These maps are based on the increasing amount of primary source material now available, describing the Soviet economy. Starting in the mid-1950s, a large volume of information has been published by the Soviet government in descriptive, statistical, and cartographic form. In addition, Soviet journals, both scientific and popular, continue to publish up-to-date information on many spatial aspects of the Soviet economy. We have also relied on current journals published outside the Soviet Union for studies that provide such information.

The Soviet government has, in the more than half-century of its existence, repeatedly overhauled the spatial-administrative structure of the economy. The fifteen economic regions portrayed here represent, we believe, a division which has been widely adopted by students of the Soviet economy, and which offers the added advantage of conforming in many respects to the long-range aspects of regional planning, as practiced in the Soviet Union since 1927.

The maps of this atlas consist of two groups: four general maps, and sixty regional maps. The general maps that form the introductory section of the atlas show spatial patterns for the entire Soviet Union. The vegetation map portrays the eight principal vegetation zones which, in turn, reflect the distribution of soils, surface features, and climate, all important physical determinants of patterns of farming. The map of major administrative divisions locates the fifteen Soviet Republics that compose the Union of Soviet Socialist Republics and their important subdivisions, thus illustrating the federal structure of the nation and underlining the spatial basis of its economic plans. The third map provides an overall view of the domestic operations of AEROFLOT, the Soviet civil airline; air transport is fast gaining in importance as the most rapid means of transport in the immense space of the Soviet Union. The last overall map is one of population densities, based on the 1959 census, the latest for which detailed information is available.

The main section of the atlas consists of sixty regional maps, divided into fifteen groups of four, each portraying in detail one major region of the Soviet Union. The first map in each group shows agriculture and land use: principal crop combinations, stock raising, the use of forests, hunting, trapping, and fishing. The second map in each series is of mining and of minerals: major deposits known, centers of exploitation, gas and oil pipelines, and refineries. The third map portrays industry, while the fourth shows surface transport by rail, road, and water and indicates the size of urban centers. Railroads are drawn in a generalized form, showing all lines known to be in operation except industrial spurs.

In the years since the first edition of this atlas in 1960, certain changes have taken place in the Soviet Union. The preliminary results of the 1970 census indicate that the Soviet population then stood at 242 million: 56 percent of the Soviet people now live in urban centers, as compared with 48 percent in 1959. This statistic underlines the importance of the industrial, transportation, and service functions now performed by Soviet cities and towns. Most of the changes registered in this atlas, as compared with the first edition of 1960, deal with shifts in the structure of urban centers, the addition of new towns of importance, and the further diversification of industry in towns already in existence a decade ago.

Perhaps the most important change in the structure of the Soviet economy during the past decade has been the increase in importance of hydrocarbons in the energy supply; accordingly, one of the most important sources consulted was a work edited by H. B. Mel'nikov: *Toplivno-Energeticheskie Resursii* (Moscow, 1968). For an overall survey of spatial shifts of the economy, we turned to A. N. Lavrishchev's *Ekonomicheskaya Geografiya SSSR* (Moscow, 1967). The excellent encyclopedic work, *Kratkaya Geograficheskaya Ensiklopediya,* 5 vols. (Moscow, 1960–66), published under the general editorship of A. A. Grigor'ev, provided a wealth of detailed information, supported by maps and statistics. Constant use was made of the statistical handbook, now published yearly, *Narodnoye Khozaystvo SSSR,* and of the statistical abstract *SSSR v Tsifrakh.*

Two major cartographic works, published during the 1960s, provided much help: a general atlas of the Soviet Union, *Atlas SSSR* (Moscow, 1962), and the jubilee atlas, summing up economic and cultural accomplishments of half a century of Soviet rule, *Atlas Razvitiya Khozyaistva i Kul'turii SSSR* (Moscow, 1967).

Current periodicals consulted include *Soviet Geography: Review and Translation* (New York); *Current Digest of the Soviet Press* (New York); *Geografiya v Shkole;* and the principal geographical periodicals of the United States, Great Britain, and the Soviet Union.

The work of preparing this revised edition was supported by a generous grant from the Faculty Research Fund of the Horace H. Rackham School of Graduate Studies of the University of Michigan. The author is pleased to acknowledge the invaluable assistance of Miss Holly Fry, Research Assistant, and of Mrs. Betty Bellaire, Cartographer, who prepared the original maps, and corrected, redrafted, and revised them for this edition.

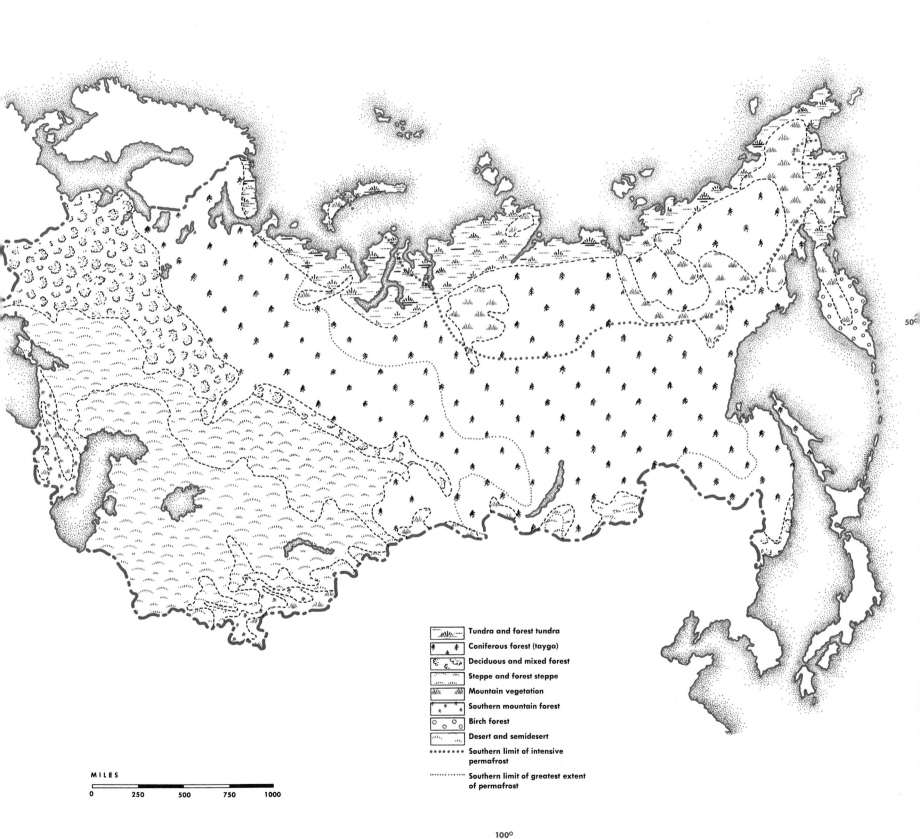

100°

50°

Tundra and forest tundra

Coniferous forest (tayga)

Deciduous and mixed forest

Steppe and forest steppe

Mountain vegetation

Southern mountain forest

Birch forest

Desert and semidesert

•••••• Southern limit of intensive permafrost

·········· Southern limit of greatest extent of permafrost

MILES

0   250   500   750   1000

100°

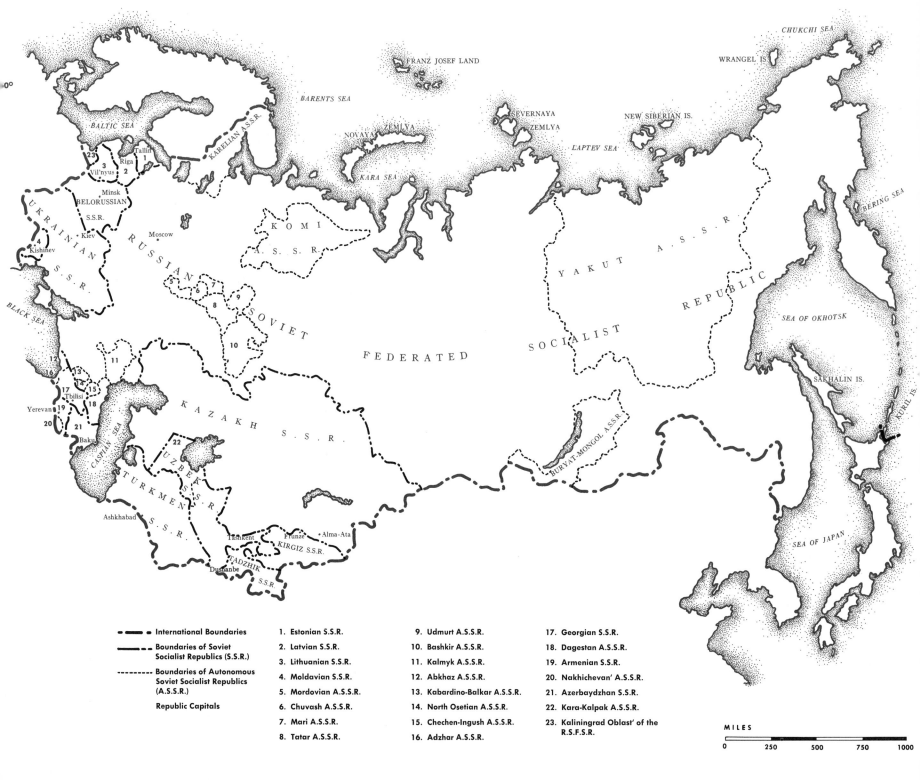

100°

CHUKCHI SEA

FRANZ JOSEF LAND

WRANGEL IS.

BARENTS SEA

NEW SIBERIAN IS.

SEVERNAYA
ZEMLYA

BALTIC SEA

NOVAYA ZEMLYA

L'APTEV SEA

BERING SEA

KARELIAN A.S.S.R.

KARA SEA

Tallin 1

Riga

3

Vil'nyus 2

23

Minsk
BELORUSSIAN

KOMI

A. S. S. R.

YAKUT A. S. S. R.

S.S.R.

Kiev

Moscow

UKRAINIAN

RUSSIAN

SEA OF OKHOTSK

4

Kishinev

S. S. R.

5

7

SOVIET

REPUBLIC

6

BLACK SEA

9

8

SOCIALIST

SAKHALIN IS.

10

FEDERATED

12

11

KURIL IS.

6

13

SEA OF JAPAN

14

KAZAKH S. S. R.

17 15

Tbilisi 18

Yerevan 19

20

21

CASPIAN SEA

Baku

22

UZBEK S.S.R.

BURYAT-MONGOL A.S.S.R.

TURKMEN S. S. R.

Ashkhabad

Tashkent

Frunze • Alma-Ata

KIRGIZ S.S.R.

TADZHIK

Dushanbe

S. S. R.

—·—·—·— International Boundaries

1. Estonian S.S.R.

9. Udmurt A.S.S.R.

17. Georgian S.S.R.

———·— Boundaries of Soviet
Socialist Republics (S.S.R.)

2. Latvian S.S.R.

10. Bashkir A.S.S.R.

18. Dagestan A.S.S.R.

3. Lithuanian S.S.R.

11. Kalmyk A.S.S.R.

19. Armenian S.S.R.

- - - - - Boundaries of Autonomous
Soviet Socialist Republics
(A.S.S.R.)

4. Moldavian S.S.R.

12. Abkhaz A.S.S.R.

20. Nakhichevan' A.S.S.R.

5. Mordovian A.S.S.R.

13. Kabardino-Balkar A.S.S.R.

21. Azerbaydzhan S.S.R.

Republic Capitals

6. Chuvash A.S.S.R.

14. North Osetian A.S.S.R.

22. Kara-Kalpak A.S.S.R.

7. Mari A.S.S.R.

15. Chechen-Ingush A.S.S.R.

23. Kaliningrad Oblast' of the
R.S.F.S.R.

8. Tatar A.S.S.R.

16. Adzhar A.S.S.R.

MILES

0   250   500   750   1000

100°

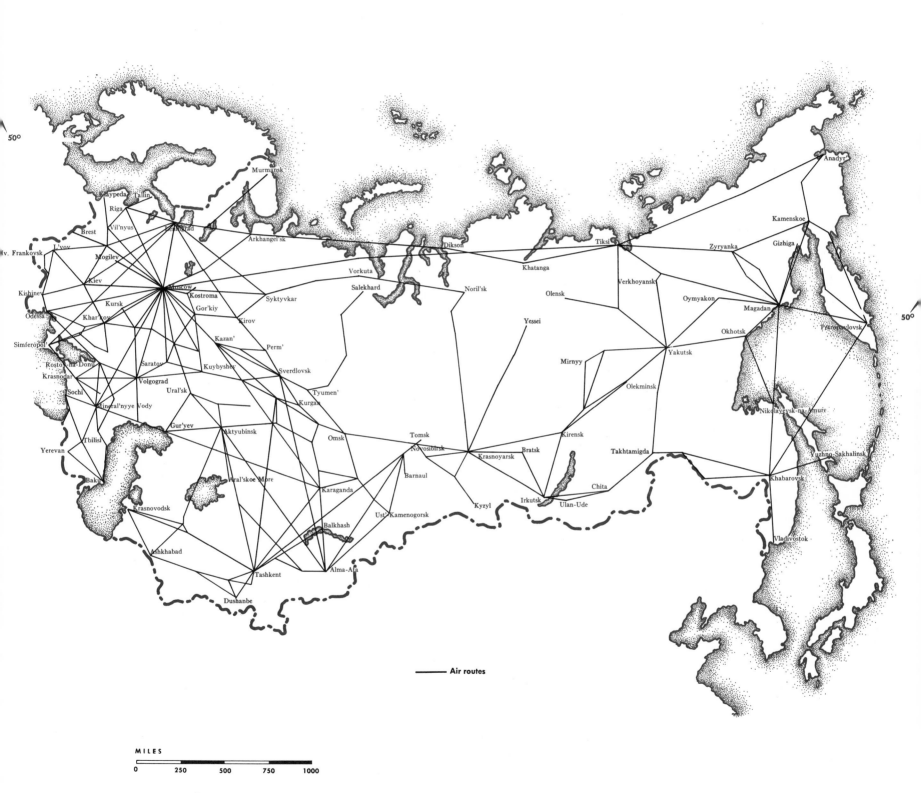

100°

50°

50°

Murmansk
Klaypeda
Tallin
Riga
Vil'nyus
Brest
Leningrad
Arkhangel'sk
Dikson
Tiksi
Zyryanka
Gizhiga
Kamenskoe
Anadyr'
lv. Frankovsk
L'voy
Mogilev
Kiev
Kishinev
Moscow
Kostroma
Syktyvkar
Vorkuta
Salekhard
Noril'sk
Khatanga
Verkhoyansk
Olensk
Oymyakon
Magadan
Yessei
Okhotsk
Petropavlovsk
Odessa
Kursk
Khar'kov
Gor'kiy
Kirov
Simferopol'
Kazan'
Perm'
Rostou-na-Donu
Saratov
Kuybyshev
Sverdlovsk
Yakutsk
Krasnodar
Volgograd
Ural'sk
Tyumen'
Mirnyy
Sochi
Mineral'nyye Vody
Kurgan
Olekminsk
Nikolayevsk-na-Amure
Tbilisi
Gur'yev
Aktyubinsk
Omsk
Tomsk
Kirensk
Takhtamigda
Yuzhno-Sakhalinsk
Yerevan
Novosibirsk
Krasnoyarsk
Bratsk
Baku
Ural'skoe More
Barnaul
Khabarovsk
Krasnovodsk
Karaganda
Kyzyl
Irkutsk
Chita
Ulan-Ude
Ashkhabad
Ust'-Kamenogorsk
Balkhash
Vladivostok
Tashkent
Alma-Ata
Dushanbe

——— Air routes

MILES

0   250   500   750   1000

100°

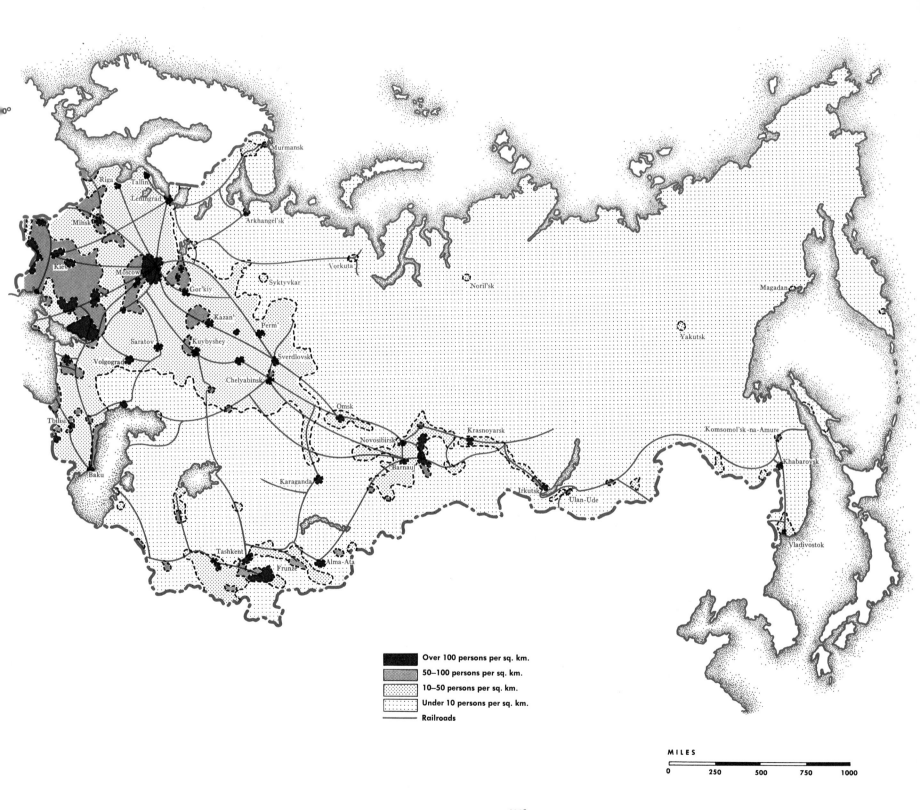

Over 100 persons per sq. km.

50–100 persons per sq. km.

10–50 persons per sq. km.

Under 10 persons per sq. km.

Railroads

MILES

0   250   500   750   1000

Central Region

The Central Region is the political and administrative core of the Soviet Union. Here, between the Volga and Oka rivers, took place the rebirth of the Russian state after the Mongol invasion. Moscow, the largest city of the region, became Russia's capital during the fourteenth century. Although overshadowed by St. Petersburg (Leningrad) during the eighteenth and nineteenth centuries, Moscow remained even then the traditional center of all Russia; since 1918 it has developed into a metropolis of over six million people, the federal capital of the country once again.

The Central Region is part of the Russian plain; it is flat to gently rolling country. Originally wooded for the most part, it has never been a leading agricultural region, yet the ease of communications, especially by waterways, and the presence of court and nobility in and around Moscow has favored the development of artisan industries since medieval times. In the mid-nineteenth century Moscow became the hub of the railroads of European Russia; at present eleven trunk railroads connect the city with all parts of the USSR. Inland waterways, such as the Moscow–Volga and Don–Volga canals, now link Moscow with the Caspian Sea as well as the Baltic, the Sea of Azov, and the Black Sea. Existing all-weather roads connect Moscow with the Leningrad, Belorussian, and Ukrainian regions. This city is also the center of the Soviet civil aviation network.

Few if any great industrial regions of the world are as devoid of raw materials and fuels as the Central Region of the Soviet Union. The Kursk iron ore deposits, where large-scale development has only begun, and the Moscow area lignite mines are the only important local resources. Coal, oil, most of the iron ore, and all essential metals and minerals are brought from other regions of the country. The Volga hydroelectric development scheme now provides substantial amounts of electric power, but the overall industrial growth of the Central Region is based on governmental planning rather than on local resource development.

In overall industrial production, as measured by the variety and importance of its industries, the Central Region is the center of Soviet manufacturing. Textile mills, small-scale metallurgy, and machine building characterized the region prior to 1914; at present textiles remain the leading industry of several of the older cities, e.g., Ivanovo. The chief industries of the Central Region today are chemicals, fine metallurgy and machine building, and electronics. Their products range from automobiles, trucks, railroad rolling stock, and ships through machine tools and ball bearings to television and radio equipment. In terms of the total value of industrial production, the Central Region undoubtedly leads all Soviet industrial areas.

Industrialization on such a scale entails advanced urban development. Moscow is the largest city of the Soviet Union with over six million inhabitants. It is surrounded by "satellite" industrial cities and "dormitory" suburbs. The Kremlin, command post and nerve center of the Soviet Union, has retained its historic buildings, but most of the rest of Moscow has undergone large-scale urban renewal and expansion. The influence of Moscow on the political, administrative, economic, artistic, and intellectual life of the USSR is overwhelming, and the rhythm of life in the city reflects the role it plays in Soviet affairs.

Gor'kiy is second to Moscow in population. Its location at the confluence of the Volga and Oka rivers and its long-standing role as a center of fairs and commerce are reflected in its importance in the transportation and chemical industries. The other urban centers of the Central Region fall into two groups. The majority are old cities, such as Yaroslavl', Vladimir, and Tula, which were given a spur to develop by industries in the nineteenth and twentieth centuries. Others, such as Novomoskovsk, Dzerzhinsk, and Rybinsk, became industrial centers of importance during the years of the Soviet regime.

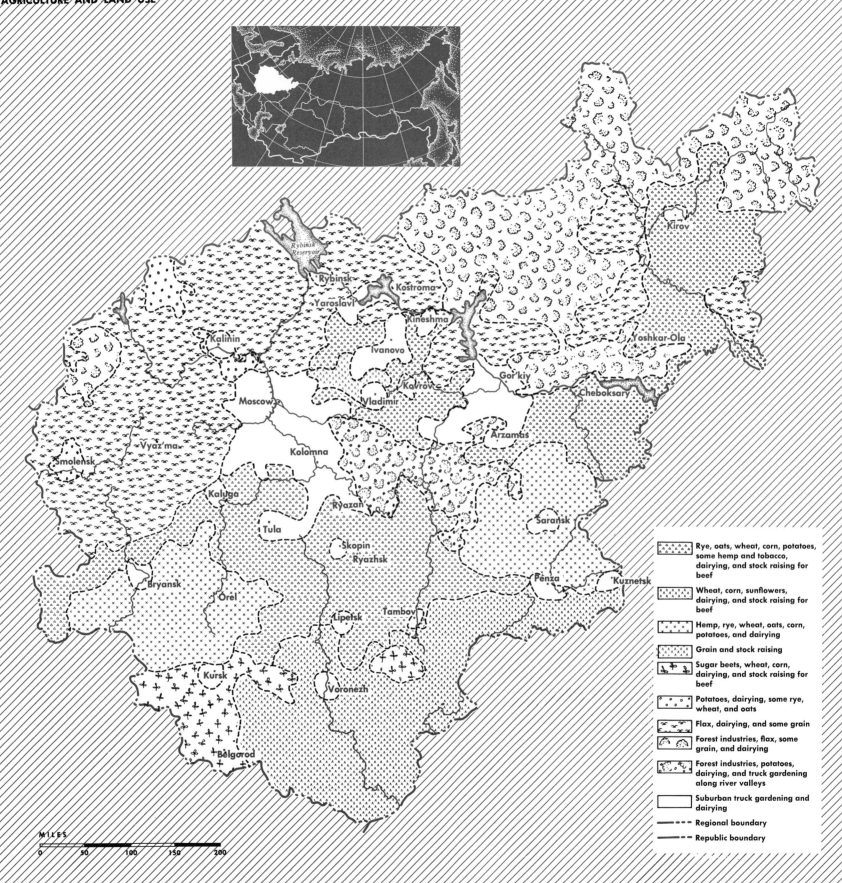

Rye, oats, wheat, corn, potatoes, some hemp and tobacco, dairying, and stock raising for beef

Wheat, corn, sunflowers, dairying, and stock raising for beef

Hemp, rye, wheat, oats, corn, potatoes, and dairying

Grain and stock raising

Sugar beets, wheat, corn, dairying, and stock raising for beef

Potatoes, dairying, some rye, wheat, and oats

Flax, dairying, and some grain

Forest industries, flax, some grain, and dairying

Forest industries, potatoes, dairying, and truck gardening along river valleys

Suburban truck gardening and dairying

Regional boundary

Republic boundary

MILES
0   50   100   150   200

Kirov
Yoshkar-Ola
Cheboksary
Rybinsk Reservoir
Rybinsk
Kostroma
Yaroslavl
Kineshma
Kalinin
Ivanovo
Gor'kiy
Kovrov
Vladimir
Moscow
Arzamas
Vyaz'ma
Kolomna
Smolensk
Kaluga
Ryazan
Saransk
Tula
Skopin
Ryazhsk
Bryansk
Penza
Kuznetsk
Orel
Tambov
Lipetsk
Kursk
Voronezh
Belgorod

Rudnichnyy

Kirov
Omutninsk

Rybinsk Reservoir

Rybinsk
Kostroma
Yaroslavl
Kineshma

VOLGA

Ostashkov
Selizharovo
Kalinin
Ivanovo
Shuya

Klin
Dmitrov
KLYAZ'MA
Gor'kiy
Cheboksary

Volokolamsk
Yuzha
VOLGA

Moscow
MOSKVA

DNEPR
Shatura
Voskresensk
OKA

Smolensk
Vyksa

Serpukhov
OKA

Ryazan
Saransk

TSNA

Tula
Cherepet
Novomoskovsk
Skopin

Bryansk
Tovarkovo

Surazh
Karachev
DESNA

Orel

Lipetsk
Tambov

DON

Shchigry

Kursk
Voronezh

Staryy Oskol

Belgorod
Nikitovka

Legend

- Lignite
- Peat
- Oil refining
- Iron ore
- P Phosphorite
- Mercury
- ▬▬ Oil pipeline
- ✗✗✗✗ Oil pipeline under construction or planned
- ──○ Gas pipeline
- ──○ Gas pipeline under construction or planned
- ········· Lignite field
- ▬ ▪ ▬ Regional boundary
- ▬ ▬ Republic boundary

40°

54°

MILES
0   50   100   150   200

Lal'sk

Rudnichnyy

Kirs

Peskovka

Omutninsk

Kotel'nich
Kirov

Buy

Neya

Manturovo

Vetluga

Rybinsk Reservoir

Rybinsk
Bezhetsk

Kostroma
Kineshma

Vyshniy Volochek
Kuvshinovo

Kimry

Yaroslavl'

Semenov

Yoshkar-Ola

Kalinin

Pereslavl'-Zalesskiy
Ivanovo
Shuya
Kovrov
Pravdinsk

Rzhev

Dmitrov

Zapadnaya Dvina

Klin
Zagorsk
Kol'chugino

Gor'kiy

Mariinskiy Posad
Volzhsk

Dzerzhinsk

Cheboksary

Smolensk
Yartsevo
Vyaz'ma

Noginsk
Vladimir
Orekhovo-Zuyevo
Lyskovo
Kozlovka

Moscow

Pavlovo

Murom
Arzamas
Shumerlya
Kanash

Podol'sk
Voskresensk
Obninsk
Serpukhov
Kolomna
Kasimov
Vyksa
Kulebaki
Pervomaysk
Alatyr

Roslavl'
Lyudinovo
Kaluga
Kashira
Ryazan'

Saransk

Tula
Mikhaylov

Kosaya Gora
Belev
Novomoskovsk
Skopin
Nizhniy Lomov
Penza

Zhizdra
Shchekino
Morshansk
Kamenka

Surazh
Bryansk
Yefremov
Michurinsk
Kirsanov
Kuznetsk

Klintsy
Novozybkov
Orel
Yelets
Tambov
Serdobsk

Lipetsk
Shchigry

Kursk
Voronezh
Borisoglebsk

Belgorod
Shebekino

	Ferrous metallurgy
	Nonferrous metallurgy
	Machinery
	Farm machinery
	Shipbuilding
	Railroad stock
	Automobile industry
	Chemicals
	Textiles
	Woodworking
	Paper
	Construction materials
	Light industry
	Thermal-electric power station
	Hydroelectric power station
	Atomic power station
---	Regional boundary
---	Republic boundary

MILES
0   50   100   150   200

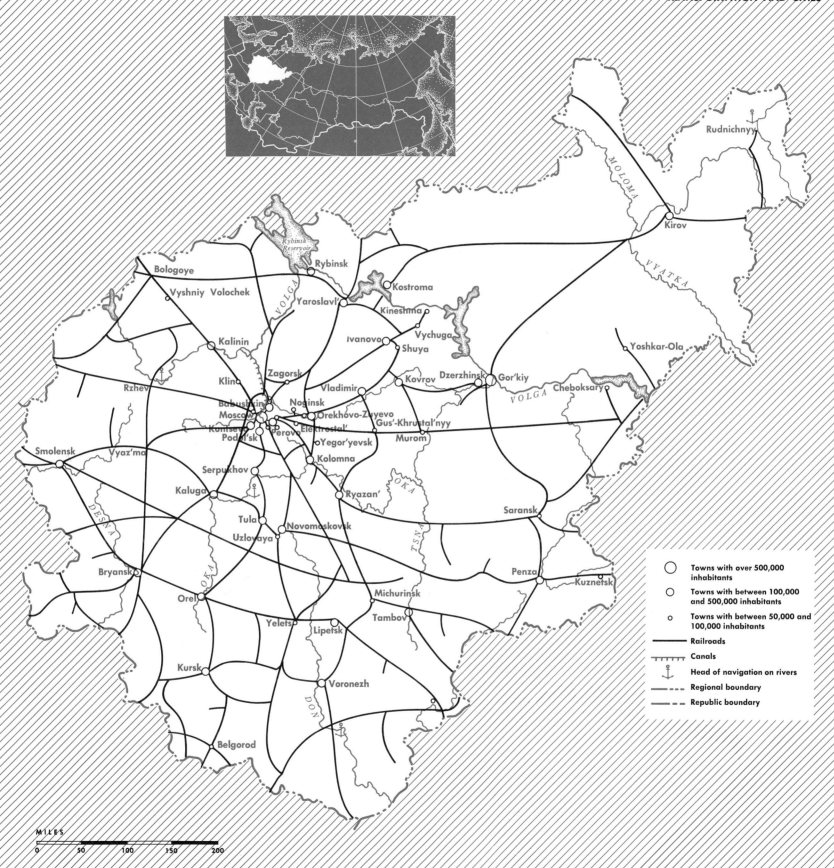

Rudnichnyy

Kirov

MOLOMA

VYATKA

Bologoye

Rybinsk Reservoir

Rybinsk

Vyshniy Volochek

VOLGA

Yaroslavl'

Kostroma

Kineshma

Kalinin

Ivanovo

Vychuga

Shuya

Yoshkar-Ola

Rzhev

Klin

Zagorsk

Vladimir

Kovrov

Dzerzhinsk

Gor'kiy

Cheboksary

VOLGA

Babushkin

Moscow

Noginsk

Orekhovo-Zuyevo

Gus'-Khrustal'nyy

Smolensk

Kuntsevo

Perovo

Elektrostal'

Podol'sk

Yegor'yevsk

Murom

OKA

Vyaz'ma

Kolomna

Serpukhov

Ryazan'

TSNA

Saransk

Kaluga

DESNA

Tula

Novomoskovsk

Uzlovaya

Penza

Kuznetsk

Bryansk

OKA

Michurinsk

Orel

Tambov

Yelets

Lipetsk

Kursk

Voronezh

DON

Belgorod

Legend:

- ◯ Towns with over 500,000 inhabitants
- ○ Towns with between 100,000 and 500,000 inhabitants
- ∘ Towns with between 50,000 and 100,000 inhabitants
- —— Railroads
- Canals
- ⚓ Head of navigation on rivers
- Regional boundary
- Republic boundary

MILES

0   50   100   150   200

Northwestern Region

The Northwestern Region has played a major part in Russian history from the earliest times to the present. Extending from the shores of the Gulf of Finland to the Arctic Ocean and the White Sea, this region has been a major thoroughfare for commerce, a pioneer industrial center, and a source of raw materials in turn.

Most of the Northwestern Region consists of glaciated hills, plains that tend to be marshy, lakes, and desolate rocky plateaus. Its location made it a major route in early days. Through this region passed the Water Road, the great early trade route of European Russia, from the Baltic and the Gulf of Finland by way of a network of rivers and lakes to the Dnepr, the Black Sea, and Byzantium. Novgorod and Pskov on the Water Road were among the earliest Russian cities, and their leadership in medieval trade was long unchallenged. The decline of the Water Road, and the parallel rise of Swedish, Polish, Lithuanian, and German power in the Baltic Sea, cut Russia off from the West. It was only later, during the reign of Peter the Great in the early eighteenth century, that St. Petersburg, the present-day Leningrad, was founded. From its beginnings it was called "Russia's window to the West."

The northern part of the Northwestern Region, providing an outlet to the ice-free waters of the westernmost Arctic Ocean, although long an area of intense missionary and fur-trading activity by the Russians, did not become an effective part of Russia until World War I.

The location of St. Petersburg at the head of the Gulf of Finland, accessible by inland as well as ocean waterways, and its role as capital during the eighteenth and nineteenth centuries, led to the rise of the city as Russia's first industrial center. Even after 1918, when Moscow was raised once more to the rank of capital of the Soviet Union, Leningrad continued to provide the cadres of industrial leadership and the critical industrial skills necessary to build modern Soviet industry.

Although now overshadowed by Moscow, Leningrad is the second largest city of the USSR, with a population of over three million. Its industries are as varied as those of the Central Region and retain a leading position in chemicals, machine tools, and electronics. Leningrad is the handsomest Soviet city—a city of palaces, churches, museums, spacious parks, and wide boulevards. It is also the shrine of the Revolution, the city where the Soviet Union was born in October–November 1917. Leningrad harbor is the busiest of the USSR and one of the main gateways to the Soviet Union.

To the south of Leningrad are Novgorod and Pskov, museum cities reminiscent of Russia's early history and of long contests with Vikings, Poles, and Swedes. To the east, Boksitogorsk with its aluminum mills and Volkhov with the first hydroelectric plant built under Soviet rule symbolize the new industrial era. To the northwest lie territories acquired from Finland in 1944, which serve as defensive screens for Leningrad.

To the north of Leningrad extend the forests and lakes of Karelia. Timber from the forest, granite and basalt for buildings, and fish from lakes and rivers and the White Sea provide the livelihood for a mixed Russian and Karelian-Finnish population. Petrozavodsk, an early center for ferrous metallurgy founded by Peter the Great in the early eighteenth century, is the only city of importance. The Baltic–White Sea Canal, connecting Leningrad with the small port of Sorokskaya, was built during the 1930s to provide a short-cut for smaller vessels bound for Arctic waters.

The northernmost part of the Northwestern Region is the Kola Peninsula, which separates the White and Barents seas and faces the Arctic Ocean. After centuries of isolation, when this district was frequented only by fishermen and reindeer herders, Kola became Russia's back door to the West with the building of the Leningrad–Murmansk railroad during World War I. In both world wars Murmansk, the only port of European Russia that is ice-free all year, played a vital role in receiving supplies from Russia's allies. It is the principal fishing port of the northern European part of the Soviet Union. Rare metals and minerals, including apatite and nepheline, mined in the Kola peninsula, support local smelting and refining industries.

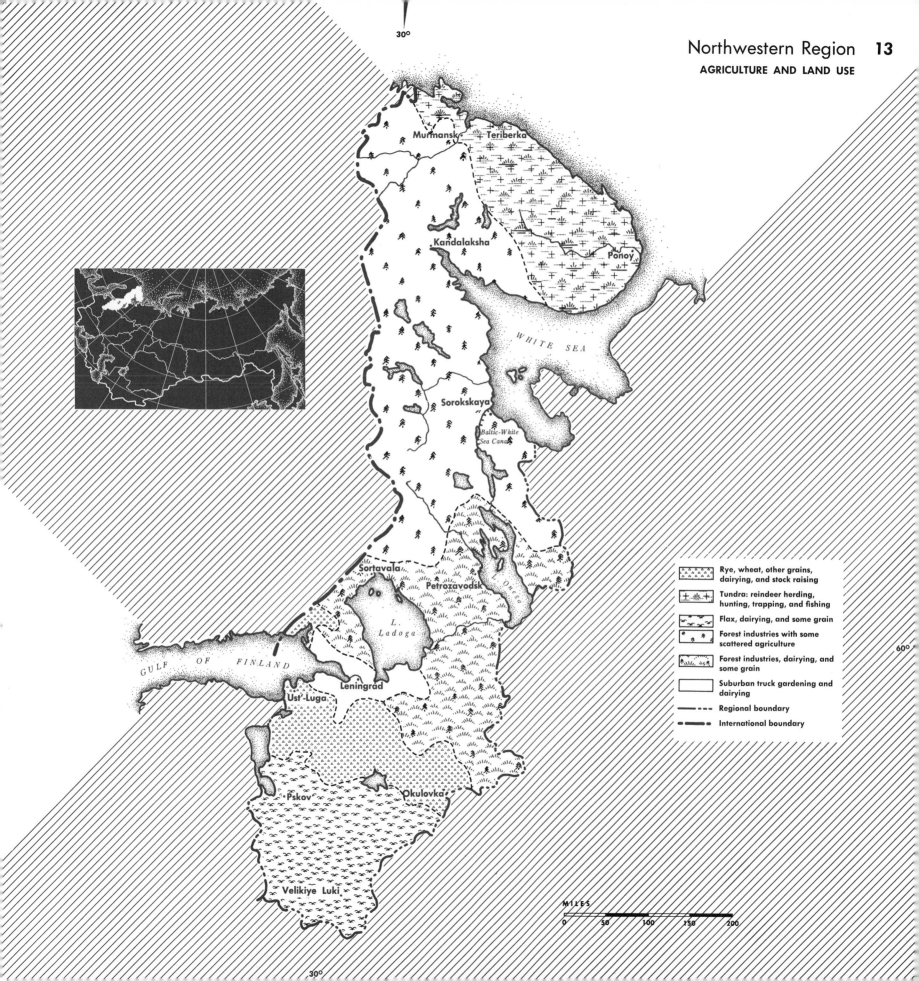

30°

30°

Murmansk
Teriberka

Kandalaksha

Ponoy

WHITE SEA

Sorokskaya

Baltic-White Sea Canal

Sortavala

Petrozavodsk

L. Onega

L. Ladoga

GULF OF FINLAND

Leningrad

Ust'-Luga

Pskov

Okulovka

Velikiye Luki

60°

Legend

- Rye, wheat, other grains, dairying, and stock raising
- Tundra: reindeer herding, hunting, trapping, and fishing
- Flax, dairying, and some grain
- Forest industries with some scattered agriculture
- Forest industries, dairying, and some grain
- Suburban truck gardening and dairying
- — · — Regional boundary
- — ▬ — International boundary

MILES
0   50   100   150   200

30°

Lignite	
Peat	
Oil shale	
Oil refining	
Cobalt	
Iron ore	
Nickel	N
Aluminum ore	AL
Copper	C
Lead, zinc, silver	
Pyrites	S
Phosphorite and apatite	P
Mica	
Building stone	
Gas pipeline	
Gas pipeline under construction or planned	
Lignite field	
Regional boundary	
International boundary	

Nikel'

TULOMA

Monchegorsk

Kirovsk

Chupa

WHITE SEA

Baltic-White Sea Canal

Medvezh'yegorsk

Kondopoga

Petrozavodsk

Pitkyaranta

L. Onega

L. Ladoga

SVIR'

GULF OF FINLAND

60°

Leningrad

Boksitogorsk

Slantsy

Gdov

Novgorod

Borovichi

Pskov

Ostrov

MILES

0   50   100   150   200

30°

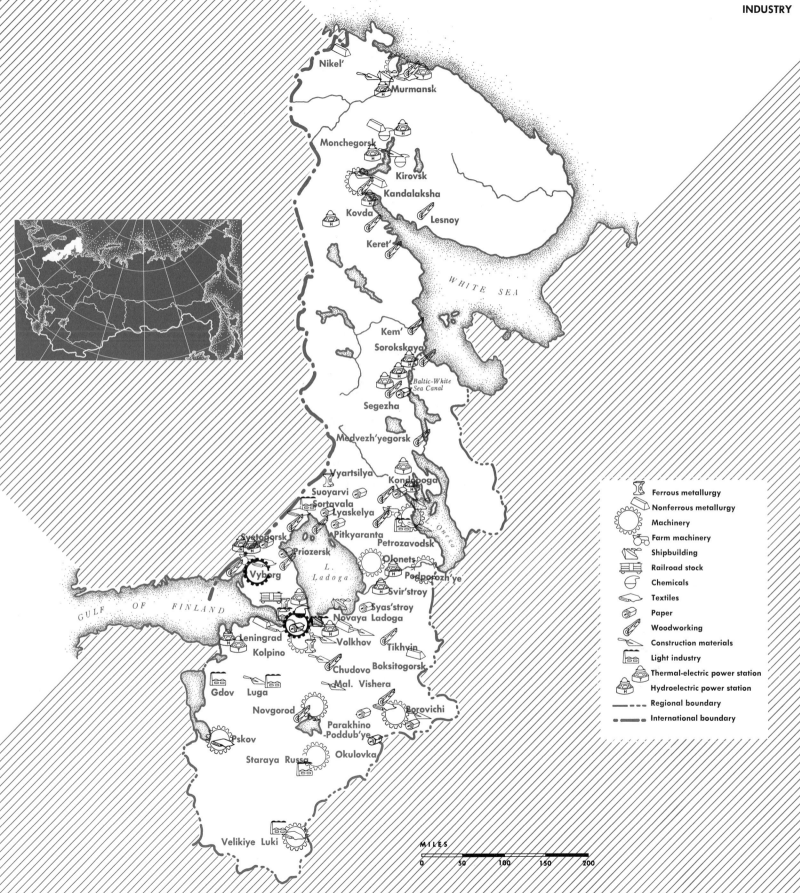

Nikel'

Murmansk

Monchegorsk

Kirovsk

Kandalaksha

Kovda

Lesnoy

Keret'

WHITE SEA

Kem'

Sorokskaya

Baltic-White Sea Canal

Segezha

Medvezh'yegorsk

Vyartsilya

Kondopoga

Suoyarvi

Sortavala

Lyaskelya

Pitkyaranta

Petrozavodsk

Svetogorsk

Priozersk

Olonets

L. Onega

Podporozh'ye

Vyborg

L. Ladoga

Svir'stroy

Syas'stroy

GULF OF FINLAND

Novaya Ladoga

Leningrad

Volkhov

Tikhvin

Kolpino

Chudovo

Boksitogorsk

Mal. Vishera

Gdov

Luga

Novgorod

Borovichi

Parakhino-Poddub'ye

Pskov

Staraya Russa

Okulovka

Velikiye Luki

	Ferrous metallurgy
	Nonferrous metallurgy
	Machinery
	Farm machinery
	Shipbuilding
	Railroad stock
	Chemicals
	Textiles
	Paper
	Woodworking
	Construction materials
	Light industry
	Thermal-electric power station
	Hydroelectric power station
	Regional boundary
	International boundary

MILES

0   50   100   150   200

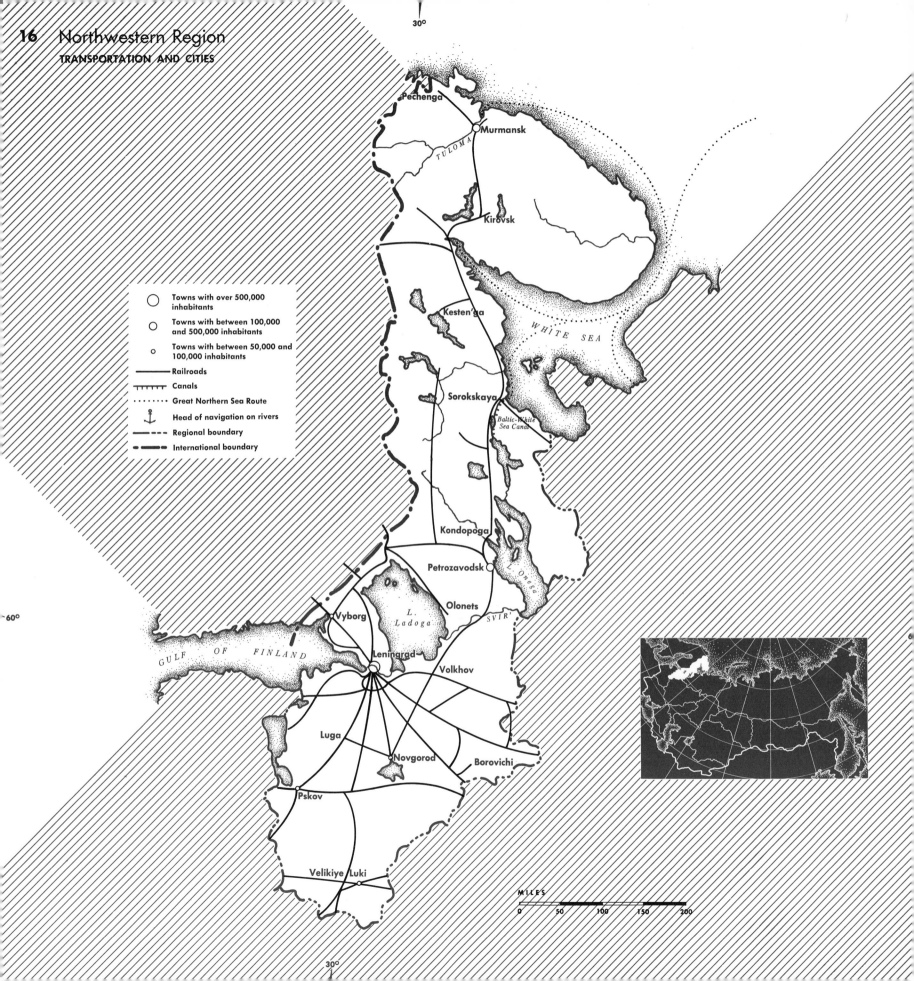

Towns with over 500,000 inhabitants

Towns with between 100,000 and 500,000 inhabitants

Towns with between 50,000 and 100,000 inhabitants

Railroads

Canals

Great Northern Sea Route

Head of navigation on rivers

Regional boundary

International boundary

30°

Pechenga

Murmansk

TULOMA

Kirovsk

WHITE SEA

Kesten'ga

Sorokskaya

*Baltic-White
Sea Canal*

Kondopoga

Petrozavodsk

L. Onega

Olonets

SVIR'

Vyborg

*L.
Ladoga*

Leningrad

Volkhov

GULF OF FINLAND

60°

Luga

Novgorod

Borovichi

Pskov

Velikiye Luki

MILES
0   50   100   150   200

30°

North European Region

From Lake Onega and the White Sea the plains and low hills of the North European Region extend nearly 800 miles eastward to the northern Urals. The Northern Dvina and Mezen' rivers in the west and the Pechora River in the east provide access to the Arctic. These three rivers were the only routes available until the building of railroads in the present century. The greater part of the region is forested, although the northern margins along the Arctic Ocean are barren tundra and the islands of Novaya Zemlya, Vaygach, Kolguyev, and Franz Josef Land are covered mostly by snow and ice.

The aboriginal inhabitants of the North European Region were conquered during the Middle Ages by the Russian city-state of Novgorod and later incorporated in the domain of Moscow. Missionaries and fur traders traversed it every winter, and the first trail to Siberia led across this region since the easier, southern routes were still in Tatar hands. The arrival of English traders during the sixteenth century and the eagerness of the Moscow government to trade with Western Europe made the North European Region's principal port, Arkhangel'sk, Russia's leading port for two hundred years, until the founding of St. Petersburg. The modern-day history of the region, however, is inseparably bound with lumbering.

The timber resources of the North European Region, while exceeded in quantity by those of Siberia, are the most accessible of the Soviet Union. For more than four decades this region has been the country's greatest producer of timber and one of the leading centers for paper, pulp, and other wood products. The streams of the Northern Dvina, Mezen', and Pechora drainage systems provide excellent waterways for the floating of timber to pulp mills. Two railroads connect the area with the Central Region further south. The Vologda–Arkhangel'sk line was built during the early years of the twentieth century, and the Kotlas–Vorkuta line was completed shortly before the outbreak of World War II. Wood and wood products of this region also benefit from the available ocean shipping, especially from the port of Arkhangel'sk. From Arkhangel'sk ships ply to the ports of Western Europe, as well as to the outposts along the Great Northern Sea Route which connects the European shores of the USSR by way of the Arctic Ocean with the Bering Sea and the Pacific.

Forestry is the dominant form of land utilization. Grain, potatoes, and flax are grown in small quantities along the southern margins of the region. Nearly everywhere else farms are merely clearings in the wide expanse of forest. Besides cattle and pigs, reindeer herds play a part in animal husbandry. Trapping, long an important source of income of the native Komi and Nentsi tribesmen, has declined compared with Siberia.

The Pechora Basin has, in recent years, become a major source of fuels, especially coal. Vorkuta, located north of the Arctic Circle, is the center of a group of coal mines. From here the coal is shipped south, to the Central Region. It is also available for Arctic shipping by way of the branch line connecting the Vorkuta–Kotlas railroad with the lower Ob' River. Oil is produced at Ukhta, and there are some wells of natural gas.

Arkhangel'sk, at the mouth of the Northern Dvina River, is the leading city of the North European Region. Besides being a great port, especially for products of the forest industries, it also has good rail connections with Moscow to the south and with the Northwestern Region to the southwest. Its sawmills are the greatest in the USSR. Severodvinsk, across the Dvina from Arkhangel'sk, is one of the world's great timber export ports.

Vologda, the oldest city of the region, is its most important railroad junction; here the Leningrad–Kirov–Urals and Moscow–Arkhangel'sk lines cross. The city has also long been known as one of the Soviet Union's centers of dairying and for its dairy products.

Nar'yan-Mar, at the mouth of the Pechora, is a port of call of the Great Northern Sea Route. Syktyvkar, in the southern part of the region, is the administrative center of the Komi Autonomous Republic.

440

Tundra: reindeer herding, hunting, trapping, and fishing

Forest industries, dairying, and some grain

Forest industries with some scattered agriculture

Flax and dairying

Suburban truck gardening

--- ·--- Regional boundary

VAYGACH IS.

KOLGUYEV IS.

Vorkuta

Nar'yan-Mar

Indiga

WHITE SEA

Arkhangel'sk

Ukhta

64°

Syktyvkar

Vel'sk

Kotlas

Vologda

MILES

0   50   100   150   200

440

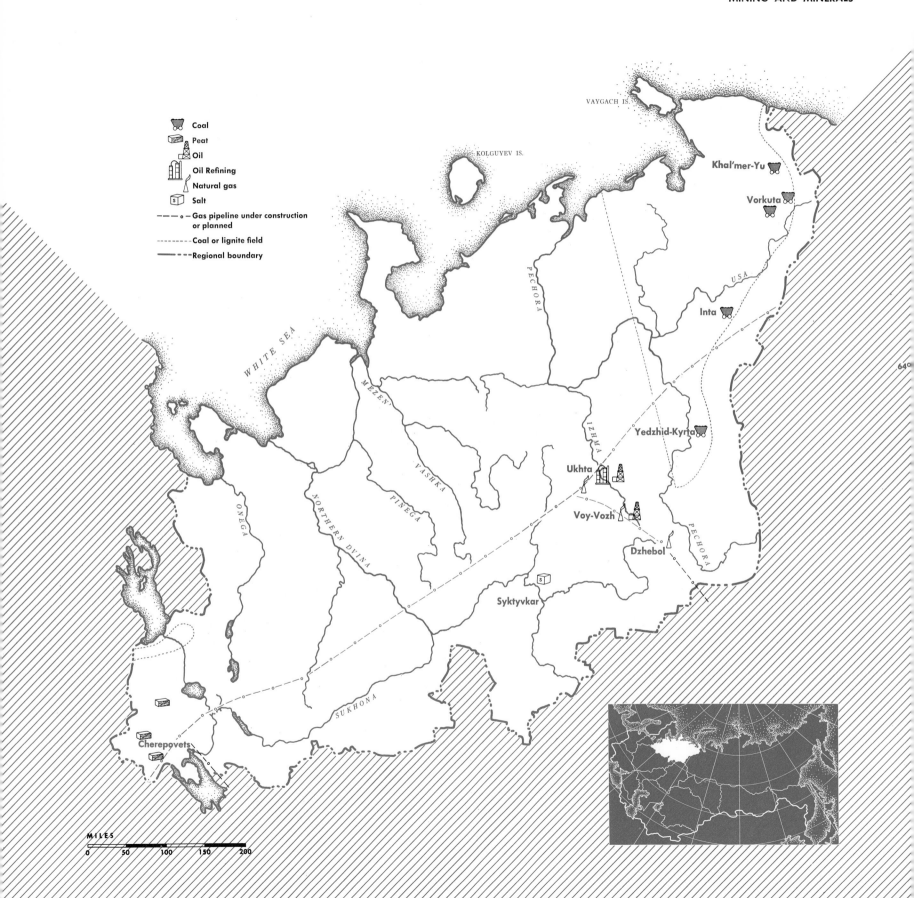

Coal

Peat

Oil

Oil Refining

Natural gas

Salt

— · — ○ — Gas pipeline under construction or planned

············ Coal or lignite field

— · · — Regional boundary

VAYGACH IS.

KOLGUYEV IS.

Khal'mer-Yu

Vorkuta

PECHORA

USA

Inta

IZHMA

Yedzhid-Kyrta

Ukhta

Voy-Vozh

PECHORA

Dzhebol

WHITE SEA

MEZEN

VASHKA

PINEGA

ONEGA

NORTHERN DVINA

S

Syktyvkar

SUKHONA

Cherepovets

MILES

0   50   100   150   200

Chemicals
Ferrous Metallurgy
Machinery
Farm machinery
Shipbuilding
Textiles
Paper
Woodworking
Construction materials
Light industry
Thermal-electric power station
Hydroelectric power station
Regional boundary

VAYGACH IS.

KOLGUYEV IS.

WHITE SEA

Vorkuta

Nar'yan-Mar

Inta

Mezen'

Shchel'yayur

Pechora

Ust'-Tsil'ma

Severodvinsk

Arkhangel'sk

Ukhta

Troitsko-Pechorsk

Onega

Samoded

Plesetsk

Mikun'

Zheleznodorozhnyy

Zheshart

Nyandoma

Syktyvkar

Kotlas

Verkhniy Rubezh

Krasavino

Velikiy Ustyug

Tot'ma

Sokol

Cherepovets

Chagoda

Vologda

MILES
0   50   100   150   200

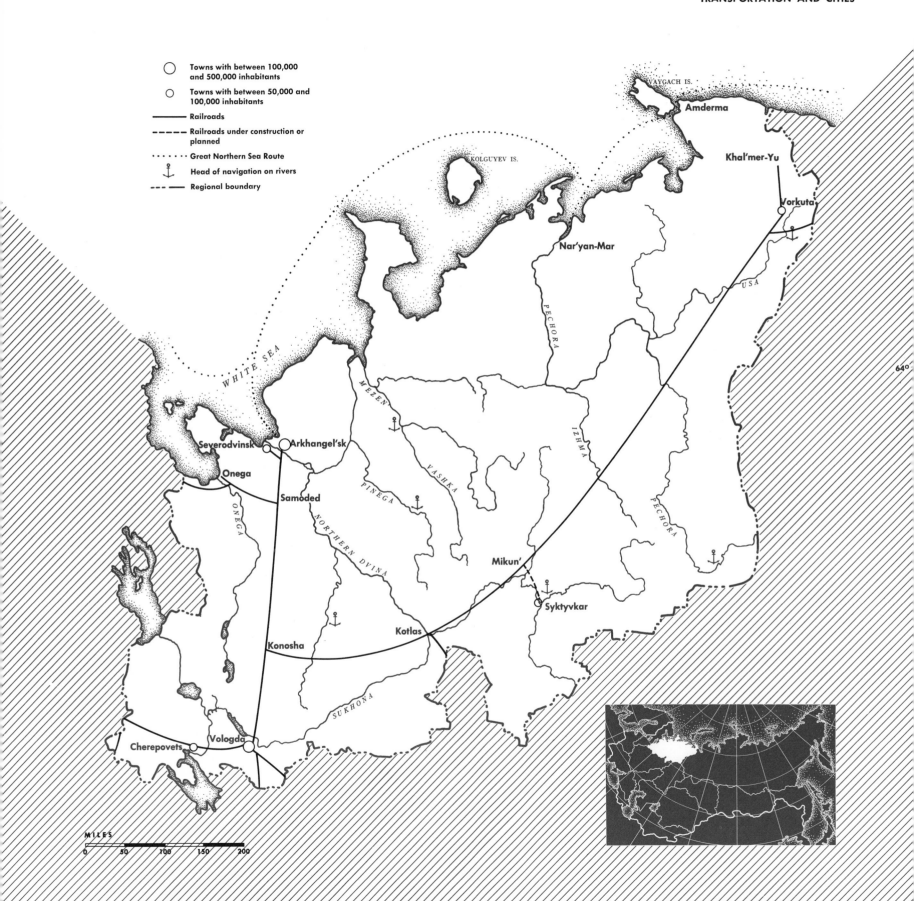

44°

VAYGACH IS.

Amderma

KOLGUYEV IS.

Khal'mer-Yu

Vorkuta

Nar'yan-Mar

PECHORA

U S A

64°

WHITE SEA

MEZEN

VASHKA

IZHMA

Severodvinsk

Arkhangel'sk

PINEGA

PECHORA

Onega

Samoded

ONEGA

NORTHERN DVINA

Mikun'

Syktyvkar

Konosha

Kotlas

SUKHONA

Cherepovets

Vologda

MILES

0   50   100   150   200

Western Region

The four Soviet Republics that constitute the Western Region, the Belorussian, Lithuanian, Latvian, and Estonian Republics, are sometimes referred to as the "western borderlands" of the Soviet Union. Since late medieval times the most important routes between Russia and the rest of Europe passed through this region, and its seaports along the Baltic lead among all Soviet ports in volume of traffic.

Although most of this region consists of plains or low hills, there is considerable variety in its landscape, due to differences in drainage and in vegetation. In the south the Pripyat' Marshes, the largest in Europe, separate Belorussia from the Ukraine. In the central part the low Belorussian Hills provide the main route from Moscow to Poland and Germany. In the north the Baltic Republics display low morainic hills, gently rolling plains, and many miles of low, sandy coast, rising towards the north to the cliffs of the Estonian coast. Forest, marsh, and bog covered the region in its primeval state, and parts of it still remain nearly untouched by the hand of man.

Belorussia ("White" Russia), in the southern part of the Western Region, was thus named in the Middle Ages to distinguish it from Muscovite, or "Red" Russia. Long an area of dispute between Russia and its western neighbors, Belorussia often changed hands, passing from Polish and Lithuanian to Russian control more than once in its stormy history. The traditional route from the West to Moscow, through Minsk, was the invasion route of Napoleon and Hitler, and it is followed by the Moscow–Minsk–Warsaw highway and railroad.

Lithuania, alone among the Baltic Soviet Republics, has played a role of great power in the past. Estonia and Latvia have known German, Swedish, and Russian rule during the past seven centuries. Following World War I the Baltic Republics obtained their independence and for twenty years led their own national existence. In 1940 all three were once more absorbed by the Soviet Union.

Agriculture in the Western Region is characterized by a limited range of crops and by the importance of forest industries. Flax and potatoes are the leading crops, utilized as vital raw materials for linen textiles, alcohol, and chemicals, as well as food and feed. There are flourishing dairy farms, and pigs are raised in large numbers.

Besides wood and building materials, oil shale is the principal raw material of importance. The oil shale deposits of Estonia are among the largest in Europe, and gas manufactured from these deposits is pumped through a pipeline to Leningrad. Peat and running water are both used to generate electric power.

Minsk, capital of the Belorussian Republic and its only large city, has long been the gateway to Russia from the West. It has a variety of industries, of which printing and the building of trucks and construction machinery are the most important. Estonia and Latvia are the important industrial areas among the Baltic Republics, their industries having been established largely prior to World War I and during the period between the two world wars.

Textiles, electronics, shipbuilding, the manufacture of precision machinery, and optics are among the more important industries of the Baltic Republics. Tallin, the capital of Estonia, is also its largest seaport. Tartu, in the southeastern part of the republic, is the seat of an old and important university; Narva, in the northeast, is Estonia's largest textile center.

Riga, on the Western Dvina (Daugava) River where it reaches the Gulf of Riga, is one of the oldest cities of the Soviet Baltic, the capital of the Latvian Soviet Republic, and its greatest industrial center. It is also a major seaport, and its airfield handles traffic with Scandinavia and Western Europe. Liepaya and Ventspils, on the open Baltic, were developed as ports by Russia prior to 1914 and served as outlets for wheat and other farm products of the Ukraine, a role still fulfilled today.

Vil'nyus, the capital of the Lithuanian Soviet Republic, on the upper Neman River, is its leading intellectual center; Kaunas, the only industrial city of importance; and Klaypeda, the republic's only seaport.

Following World War II, the Soviet Union occupied the northernmost segment of East Prussia, formerly German territory, including the Baltic port of Kaliningrad. This territory is administered directly by the Russian Federated Republic.

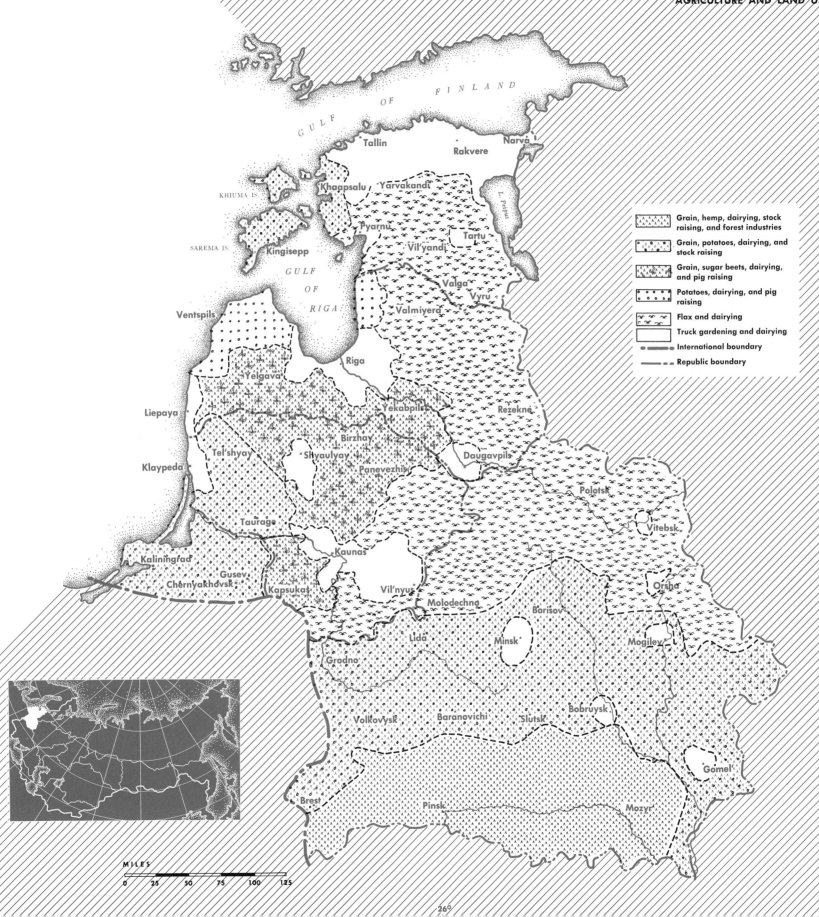

GULF OF FINLAND

Tallin
Rakvere
Narva

Khaapsalu
Yarvakandi

KHIUMA IS.

Pyarnu

L. Peipus

Vil'yandi
Tartu

SAREMA IS.

Kingisepp

GULF
OF
RIGA

Valga
Vyru

Valmiyera

Ventspils

Riga

Yelgava

Liepaya

Yekabpils

Rezekne

Tel'shyay
Birzhay
Shyaulyay
Panevezhis
Daugavpils

Klaypeda

Polotsk

Taurage

Vitebsk

Kaunas

Kalininfgrad
Gusev
Chernyakhovsk
Kapsukas
Vil'nyus
Orsha

Molodechno
Borisov

Lida
Mogilev
Minsk

Grodno

Bobruysk

Volkovysk
Baranovichi
Slutsk

Gomel'

Brest
Pinsk
Mozyr

	Grain, hemp, dairying, stock raising, and forest industries
	Grain, potatoes, dairying, and stock raising
	Grain, sugar beets, dairying, and pig raising
	Potatoes, dairying, and pig raising
	Flax and dairying
	Truck gardening and dairying
	International boundary
	Republic boundary

MILES
0   25   50   75   100   125

GULF OF FINLAND

allin

Narva

Kokhtla-Yarve

KHIUMA IS.

L. Peipus

SAREMA IS.

Pyarnu

Tartu

GULF
OF
RIGA

Riga

Kuldiga

C

C

WESTERN DVINA

Liepaya

Yekabpils

56°

5

Klaypeda

Shyaulyay

Polotsk

Vitebsk

NEMAN

Yantarnyy

Vil'nyus

Osintarf

Orsha

BEREZINA

C

Krichev

Minsk

Bobruysk

P

DNEPR

To Poland
E. Germany

P

S

S

Starobin

Gomel'

Pinsk

PRIPYAT'

	Peat
	Oil shale
	Oil refining
P	Potash
P	Phosphorite
S	Salt
C	Cement raw materials
	Building stone
	Amber
	Oil pipeline
	Oil pipeline under construction or planned
	Gas pipeline
	Gas pipeline under construction or planned
	International boundary
	Republic boundary

MILES

0   25   50   75   100   125

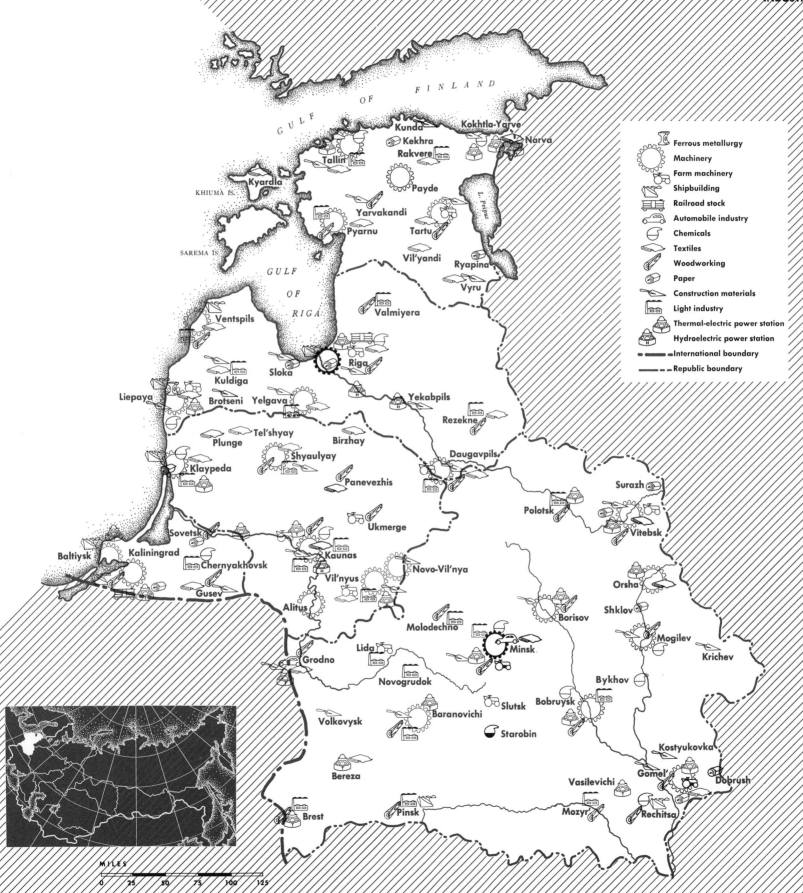

GULF OF FINLAND

KHIUMA IS.

SAREMA I.

GULF OF RIGA

L. Peipus

Legend:
- Ferrous metallurgy
- Machinery
- Farm machinery
- Shipbuilding
- Railroad stock
- Automobile industry
- Chemicals
- Textiles
- Woodworking
- Paper
- Construction materials
- Light industry
- Thermal-electric power station
- Hydroelectric power station
- ——— International boundary
- ——— Republic boundary

Kunda
Kekhra
Rakvere
Kokhtla-Yarve
Narva
Tallin
Kyardla
Payde
Yarvakandi
Pyarnu
Tartu
Vil'yandi
Ryapina
Vyru
Valmiyera
Ventspils
Sloka
Riga
Kuldiga
Yekabpils
Liepaya
Brotseni
Yelgava
Rezekne
Tel'shyay
Birzhay
Plunge
Shyaulyay
Daugavpils
Klaypeda
Panevezhis
Surazh
Polotsk
Vitebsk
Sovetsk
Ukmerge
Baltiysk
Kaliningrad
Kaunas
Novo-Vil'nya
Orsha
Chernyakhovsk
Vil'nyus
Shklov
Gusev
Borisov
Mogilev
Alitus
Molodechno
Minsk
Krichev
Lida
Grodno
Bykhov
Novogrudok
Bobruysk
Volkovysk
Baranovichi
Slutsk
Starobin
Kostyukovka
Bereza
Gomel'
Dobrush
Vasilevichi
Brest
Pinsk
Mozyr'
Rechitsa

569

26°

26°

MILES
0   25   50   75   100   125

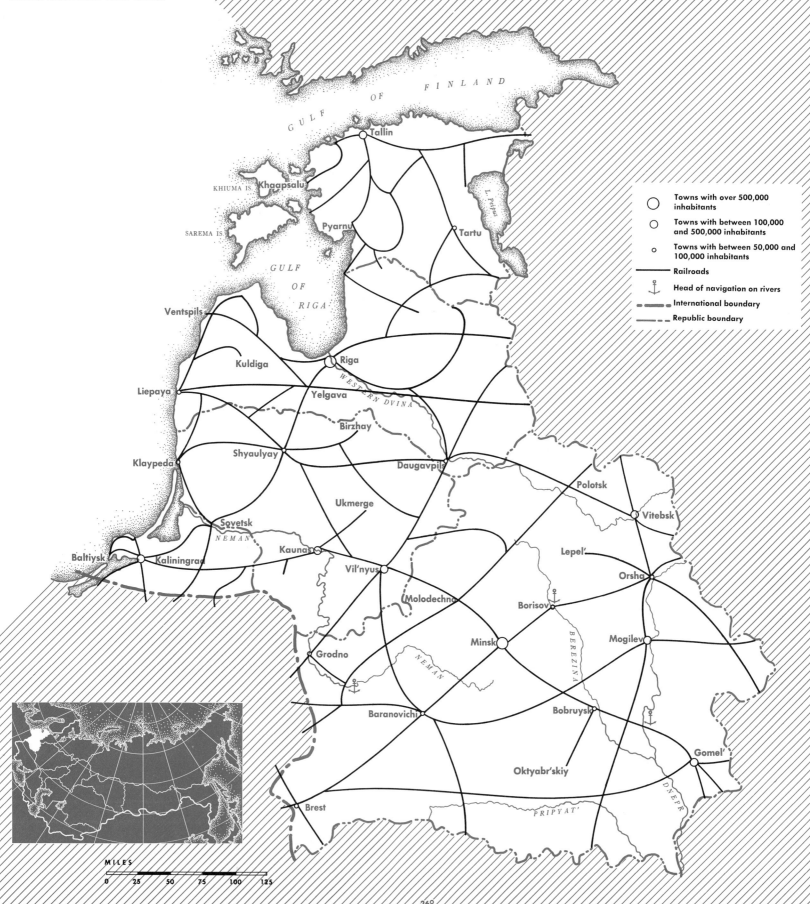

Towns with over 500,000 inhabitants

Towns with between 100,000 and 500,000 inhabitants

Towns with between 50,000 and 100,000 inhabitants

Railroads

Head of navigation on rivers

International boundary

Republic boundary

26°

GULF OF FINLAND

Tallin

KHIUMA IS.

Khaapsalu

SAREMA IS

Pyarnu

Tartu

L. Pepus

GULF OF RIGA

Ventspils

Kuldiga

Riga

WESTERN DVINA

Liepaya

Yelgava

Birzhay

56°

Shyaulyay

Daugavpils

Klaypeda

Polotsk

Ukmerge

Vitebsk

Sovetsk

NEMAN

Kaunas

Lepel'

Baltiysk

Kaliningrad

Vil'nyus

Orsha

Molodechna

Borisov

BEREZINA

Grodno

Minsk

Mogilev

NEMAN

Baranovichi

Bobruysk

Gomel'

Oktyabr'skiy

DNEPR

Brest

PRIPYAT'

MILES

0 25 50 75 100 125

26°

Southern Region

The Southern Region, comprising the Ukrainian and Moldavian Soviet Republics, is both the leading farm area of the Soviet Union and one of its principal industrial regions. The far western sector of the region includes a portion of the Carpathian Mountains and extends into the Danube Basin: its main importance is that of a transport link to Czechoslovakia and Hungary. The western half of the region is a low, rolling plateau, that slopes southward to the coastal plains of the Black Sea. The central and northern sections are mostly lowlands, rising to the low hills of the Donets Basin in the east. The Sea of Azov is a bay of the Black Sea, from which it is separated by the Crimean peninsula.

The Southern Region benefits considerably from its location and from rainfall that is adequate to ample. Except for the northern margins, where mixed forests still occupy part of the land, most of the region was a grassland in its natural state. A substantial part of the region consists of rich, deep black soils, the most fertile of the Soviet Union, ideally suited to farming. In the production of winter wheat, corn, sugar beets, and sunflowers, the Southern Region leads the Soviet Union, as in numbers of livestock of all kinds. Food industries, flour milling, sugar refining, and meat-packing, are represented in the majority of cities and towns.

Deposits of coking coal, oil, and natural gas, and large hydroelectric plants on the Dnepr River provide the energy for industrial production. Iron ore, manganese, bauxite, mercury, salt, and other metals and minerals are readily available. In addition, the Ukraine, together with the Leningrad area, was one of the first districts of Russia to know large-scale investment in heavy industry, and it benefited from the sizable manpower pool thus developed. Until the 1950s the Southern Region was the leading district of Soviet heavy industry; it now occupies second place, behind the Urals.

Three areas represent the greatest concentration of heavy industry: the great bend of the Dnepr River, between Dnepropetrovsk and Zaporozh'ye; the Donets Basin (Donbass); and the shores of the Sea of Azov. Ferrous and non-ferrous metallurgy, machine industries, and chemicals are the main branches of industrial production. Aside from these three major concentrations, Khar'kov is the single outstanding industrial center—among the most important in the Soviet machine-building and mechanical industries. Kiev, the administrative and intellectual capital of the Ukrainian Soviet Republic, plays a role in transportation and light industry. Odessa is the greatest seaport of the Southern Region, and Kherson is one of its major textile centers.

The Moldavian Soviet Republic, flanking the Ukraine in the southwest and bordering on Romania, is best known for its vineyards and orchards. Kishinev, the republic's capital, is its only sizable city. To the south of the Moldavian Republic, a southernmost extension of Ukrainian territory to the banks of the lower Danube River allows the Soviet Union control of a small sector of the Danube delta and a voice in treaties and discussions on navigation of one of Europe's great waterways.

Following World War II the Soviet Union acquired substantial territories adjacent to the Ukraine in the west, territories formerly under Polish, Romanian, and Czechoslovakian sovereignty. They are now known as the Western Ukraine (territories lying to the north of the Carpathian Mountains) and the Transcarpathian district (those lying to the south of the Carpathians). Oil and natural gas from these territories now circulate throughout European Russia, in a pipeline system that also extends beyond the Soviet boundaries to Czechoslovakia, Hungary, East Germany, and Poland.

The transportation network of the Southern Region, especially railroads, is the densest and most highly developed of the Soviet Union. Along the shores of the Black Sea, near Odessa and on the south shore of the Crimean Peninsula, are some of the most popular seaside resorts of the country.

Wheat, corn, sunflowers, some hemp, and grapes

Grain, flax, and potatoes

} Dairying and stock raising for beef

Sugar beets, wheat, some corn, and tobacco

Orchards, grapes, and tobacco

Forest industries and stock raising for meat and wool

Summer pastures and mountain forests

Suburban truck gardening and dairying

International boundary

Republic boundary

Chernigov

Sumy

Zhitomir

Kiev

Khar'kov

'vov.

Poltava

Khmel'nitskiy

Cherkassy

Vinnitsa

Chernovfsy

Kirovograd

Dnepropetrovsk

Lugansk

Krivoy Rog

Zaporozh'ye

Donetsk

Bel'tsy

Zhdanov

Kishinev

Tiraspol'

Nikolaev

Melitopol'

Bendery

Kherson

Odessa

Kagul

SEA OF AZOV

Simferopol'

BLACK SEA

MILES

0   50   100   150   200

Shostka

Novovolynsk

Sokal'

Romny

Mirgorod

Khar'kov

L'vov

Ternopol'

Poltava

Shebelinka

Izyum

Drogobych

Dashava

Khmel'nitskiy

Lisichansk

Borislav

Kalush

Zvenigorodka

Kremenchug

Slavyansk

Kadiyevka

Lugansk

Artemovsk

Krasnodon

Mukachevo

Dunayevtsy

Kirovograd

Aleksandriya

Krasnyy Luch

Solotvino

Dnepropetrovsk

Gorlovka

Chistyakovo

Zaval'ye

Donetsk

Makeyevka

Krivoy Rog

Marganets

Zaporozh'ye

Kishinev

Tokmak

Zhdanov

Nikolayev

Kherson

Odessa

DNEPR

BUG

DNESTR

DONETS

SEA OF
AZOV

Dzhankoy

Kerch'

Simferopol'

Sevastopol'

B L A C K   S E A

To Hungary
Czechoslovakia

Legend

- Coal
- Lignite
- Peat
- Oil
- Oil refining
- Natural gas
- Iron ore
- M Manganese
- MG Magnesite
- V Vanadium
- Titanium
- Mercury
- P Phosphorite
- P Potash
- S Salt
- Graphite
- AL Aluminum ore

- Oil pipeline
- Gas pipeline
- Gas pipeline under construction or planned
- Coal or lignite field
- International boundary
- Republic boundary

MILES

0   50   100   150   200

32°

48°

Shostka

Chernigov

Lutsk

Rovno

Sumy

Zhitomir

Kiev

Kanev

Poltava

Khar'kov

Berdichev

Fastov

L'vov

Cherkassy

Rubezhnoye

Ternopol'

Slavyansk

Lisichansk

Voroshilovsk

Khmel'nitskiy

Kremenchug

Dneprodzerzhinsk

Kramatorsk

Stryy

Vinnitsa

Konstantinovka

Uzhgorod

Ivano-Frankovsk

Gorlovka

Lugansk

Dunayevtsy

Uman

Mukachevo

Dnepropetrovsk

Donetsk

Kamenets-Podol'skiy

Makeyevka

Chernovtsy

Kirovograd

Soroki

Krivoy Rog

Nikopol'

Zaporozh'ye

Amvrosiyevka

Bel'tsy

Tokmak

Zhdanov

Kishinev

Berdyansk

Tiraspol'

Nikolayev

Melitopol'

Odessa

Kakhovka

Bendery

Kherson

Skadovsk

Izmail

SEA OF AZOV

Yevpatoriya

Simferopol'

Kerch

Sevastopol'

BLACK SEA

Ferrous metallurgy

Nonferrous metallurgy

Machinery

Farm machinery

Shipbuilding

Railroad stock

Automobile industry

Chemicals

Textiles

Paper

Woodworking

Construction materials

Light industry

Thermal-electric power station

Hydroelectric power station

International boundary

Republic boundary

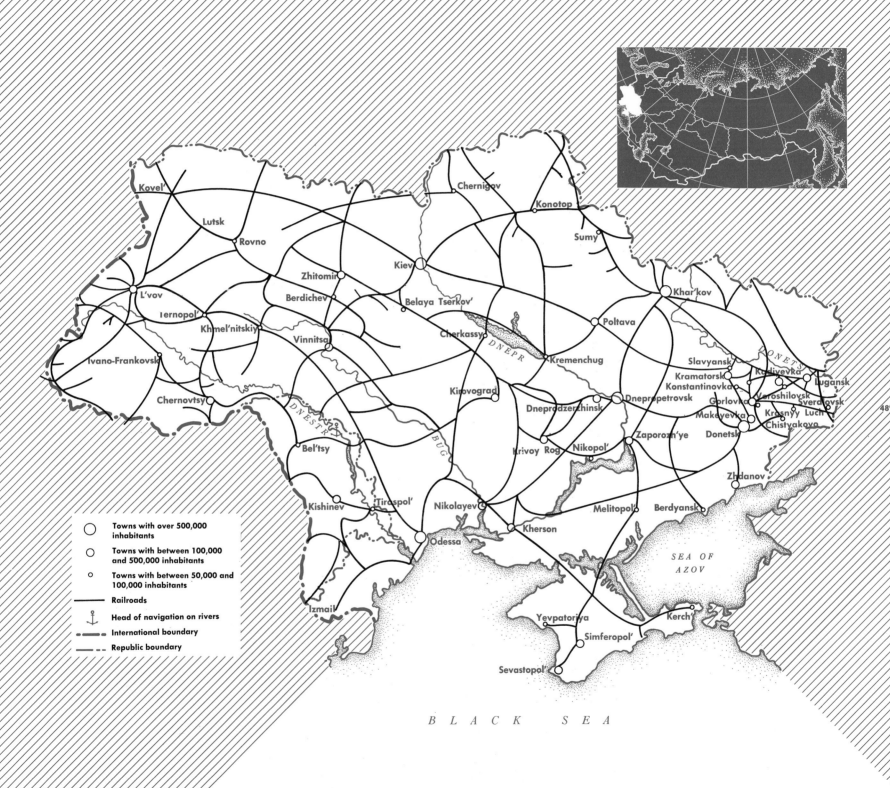

Kovel'
Lutsk
Rovno
Zhitomir
Berdichev
L'vov
Ternopol'
Khmel'nitskiy
Vinnitsa
Ivano-Frankovsk
Chernovtsy
Bel'tsy
Kishinev
Tiraspol'
Izmail
Odessa
Nikolayev
Kherson
Chernigov
Konotop
Sumy
Kiev
Belaya Tserkov'
Cherkassy
Kremenchug
Kirovograd
Krivoy Rog
Nikopol'
Zaporozh'ye
Dnepropetrovsk
Dneprodzerzhinsk
Poltava
Khar'kov
Slavyansk
Kramatorsk
Konstantinovka
Gorlovka
Makeyevka
Donetsk
Yenakiyevo
Voroshilovsk
Sverdlovsk
Krasnyy Luch
Chistyakovo
Lugansk
Melitopol'
Berdyansk
Zhdanov
Yevpatoriya
Simferopol'
Sevastopol'
Kerch'

DNEPR
DNESTR
BUG
DONETS

SEA OF AZOV

B L A C K   S E A

○ Towns with over 500,000
   inhabitants

○ Towns with between 100,000
   and 500,000 inhabitants

○ Towns with between 50,000 and
   100,000 inhabitants

— Railroads

⚓ Head of navigation on rivers

—··— International boundary

—·— Republic boundary

MILES
0   50   100   150   200

32°
48°

Volga Region

The Volga is the longest river of European Russia, its busiest waterway, and one of the principal sources of hydroelectric power of the Soviet Union. Between the city of Kazan' and the Caspian Sea, the Volga traverses forests, grasslands, and semideserts. It connects, through its tributaries and through man-made canals, the three leading industrial areas of the Soviet Union: the Central Region, the Urals, and the Southern Region.

The Volga has always been a trade route, linking the shores of the Caspian Sea with the Baltic and northern Europe. For several centuries, the river was controlled by the Tatars, until the conquest of Kazan', leading city of the middle Volga Valley, and of Astrakhan', key to the Volga delta, brought the river under Russian rule in the late 1500s. The battle of Stalingrad, the city now named Volgograd, was fought in 1943 by Soviet and German forces for control of the Volga. The Red Army's victory removed the German threat of further penetration, and turned the tide of World War II in favor of the Soviets.

From Kazan' to Volgograd, the right bank or "hill" bank of the Volga, dominated by high cliffs, stands in stark contrast to the low left bank, the "meadow" bank. Between Volgograd and the Caspian the river divides into several channels and ends in a multitude of branches, its delta, in the Caspian Sea.

The construction of large hydroelectric stations, the subsequent transformation of sections of the river into reservoirs, and the building of locks changed the whole aspect of the region, improved river navigation, and added substantially to its energy base. The hydroelectric plants at Kuybyshev and Volgograd, completed after World War II, are among the world's greatest in installed generating capacity. The Moscow–Volga and Volga–Don canals connect the river with the Soviet capital to the north, and with the Sea of Azov and the Black Sea to the south. The Kama, largest of the tributaries, provides a navigable waterway to the northwestern Urals. Even though the Volga is frozen during the winter, its huge carrying capacity for such bulk cargoes as wheat, oil, coal, and building materials makes it a vital part of the Soviet transportation system.

The middle valley, between Kazan' and Volgograd, is one of the leading producers of wheat, oil seeds, and meat in the Soviet Union. Below Volgograd, fruit, vegetables, cotton, and hemp are important crops. Fishing, especially for sturgeon, is also of importance. Flour milling, meat-packing, and cotton textiles are light industries of national significance.

The oil and gas fields of the area between the Volga and the Urals extend into the region and, with the hydroelectric power generated by the Volga, provide an important surplus of energy, fed through high-tension transmission lines and pipelines to other parts of European Russia. Oil refining is a major industry.

Kazan', where the main line of the Trans-Siberian railroad crosses the Volga, is a city of varied industries and the seat of one of the leading Soviet universities. Tol'yatti, a short distance downriver, is to become, during the decade of the 1970s, the site of the largest Soviet automobile plant. Kuybyshev's industries include petrochemical plants.

Volgograd is the principal urban and industrial center of the lower Volga region, famed for its metallurgy, farm machinery, and other mechanical industries. Astrakhan', in the Volga delta, plays a leading part in the transshipment of Caucasus oil and has important canneries processing fish and caviar.

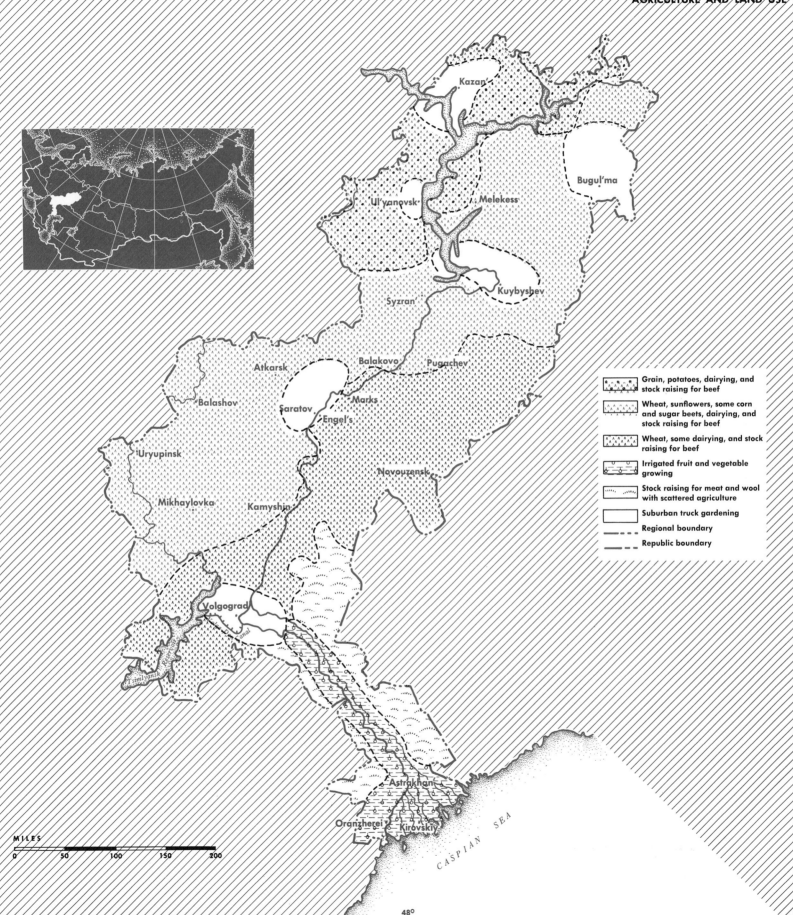

Kazan'

Bugul'ma

Ul'yanovsk
Melekess

Syzran
Kuybyshev

Atkarsk
Balakovo
Pugachev

Balashov
Saratov
Marks
Engel's

Uryupinsk
Novouzensk

Mikhaylovka
Kamyshin

Volgograd

Tsimlyansk

Astrakhan

Oranzherei
Kirovskiy

CASPIAN SEA

Grain, potatoes, dairying, and stock raising for beef

Wheat, sunflowers, some corn and sugar beets, dairying, and stock raising for beef

Wheat, some dairying, and stock raising for beef

Irrigated fruit and vegetable growing

Stock raising for meat and wool with scattered agriculture

Suburban truck gardening

Regional boundary

Republic boundary

MILES
0   50   100   150   200

MINING AND MINERALS

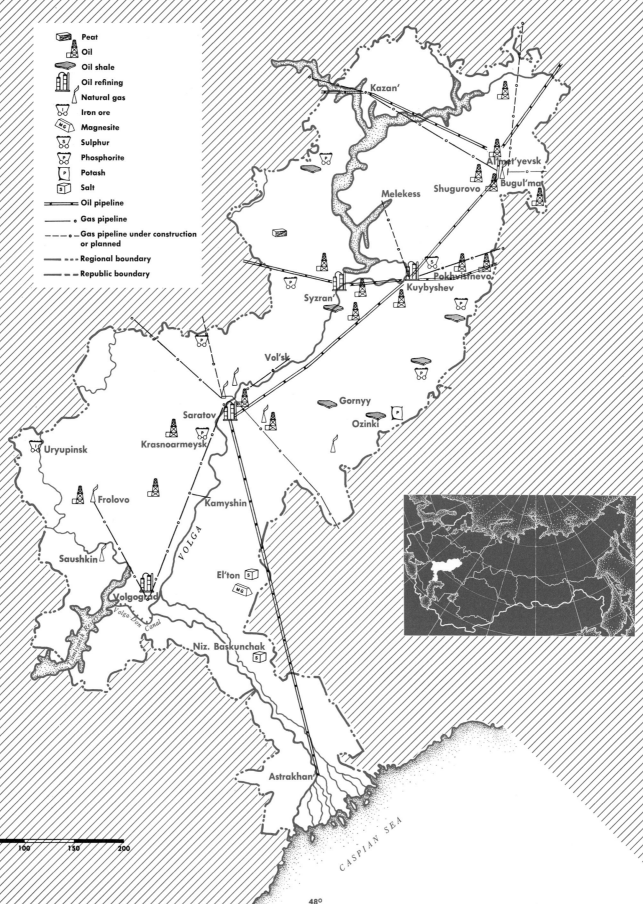

Peat
Oil
Oil shale
Oil refining
Natural gas
Iron ore
MG Magnesite
S Sulphur
Phosphorite
P Potash
S Salt
Oil pipeline
Gas pipeline
Gas pipeline under construction or planned
Regional boundary
Republic boundary

Kazan'

Al'met'yevsk
Shugurovo
Bugul'ma
Melekess

Syzran'
Kuybyshev
Pokhvistnevo

Vol'sk

Gornyy
Ozinki

Saratov

Uryupinsk
Krasnoarmeysk

Frolovo
Kamyshin

Saushkin

El'ton
VOLGA
MG

Volgograd
Volga Don Canal

Niz. Baskunchak
S

Astrakhan'

CASPIAN SEA

MILES
0   50   100   150   200

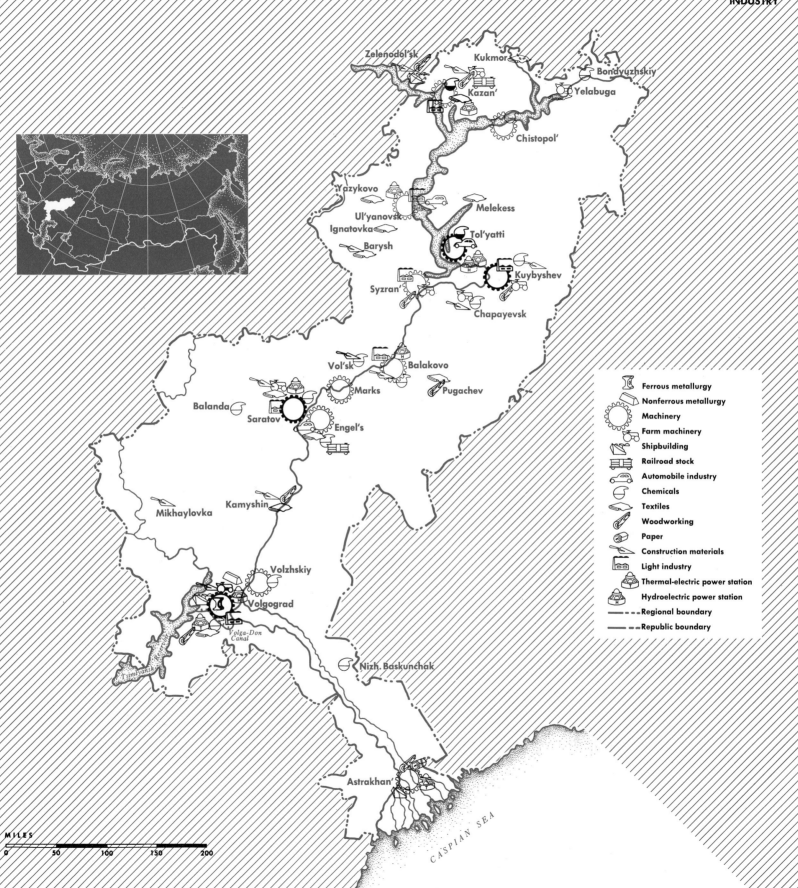

Zelenodol'sk
Kukmor
Bond'yuzhskiy
Kazan'
Yelabuga
Chistopol'
Yazykovo
Melekess
Ul'yanovsk
Ignatovka
Tol'yatti
Barysh
Kuybyshev
Syzran'
Chapayevsk
Vol'sk
Balakovo
Marks
Pugachev
Balanda
Saratov
Engel's
Mikhaylovka
Kamyshin
Volzhskiy
Volgograd
Volga-Don Canal
Tsimlyansk Res.
Nizh. Baskunchak
Astrakhan'
CASPIAN SEA

	Ferrous metallurgy
	Nonferrous metallurgy
	Machinery
	Farm machinery
	Shipbuilding
	Railroad stock
	Automobile industry
	Chemicals
	Textiles
	Woodworking
	Paper
	Construction materials
	Light industry
	Thermal-electric power station
	Hydroelectric power station
	Regional boundary
	Republic boundary

MILES

0   50   100   150   200

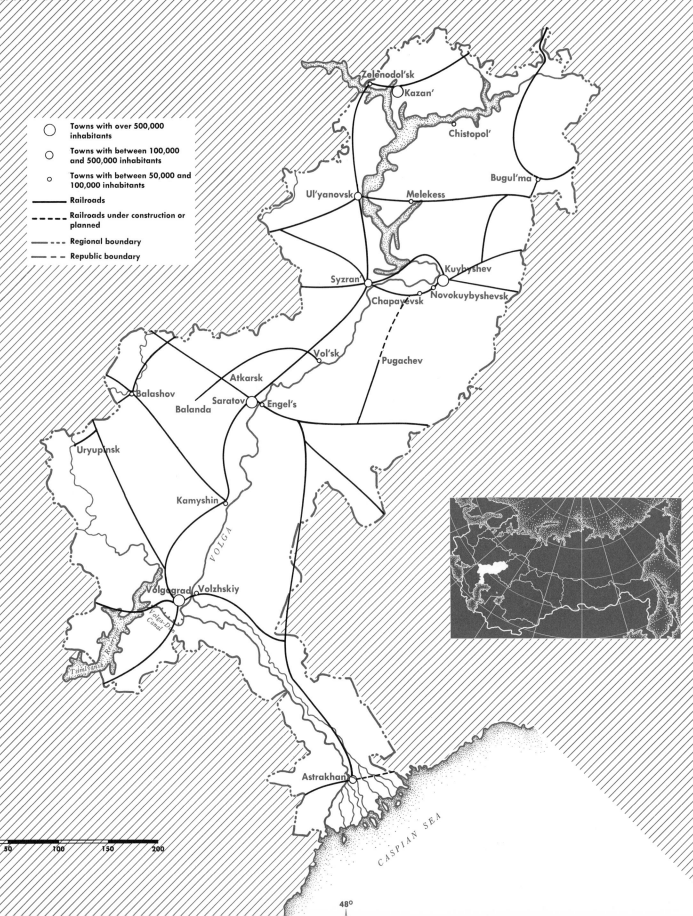

Towns with over 500,000 inhabitants

Towns with between 100,000 and 500,000 inhabitants

Towns with between 50,000 and 100,000 inhabitants

Railroads

Railroads under construction or planned

Regional boundary

Republic boundary

48°

52°

Zelenodol'sk

Kazan'

Chistopol'

Bugul'ma

Ul'yanovsk

Melekess

Syzran'

Kuybyshev

Chapayevsk

Novokuybyshevsk

Vol'sk

Pugachev

Atkarsk

Balashov

Balanda

Saratov

Engel's

Uryupinsk

Kamyshin

VOLGA

Volgograd

Volzhskiy

Volga-Don Canal

Tsimlyansk Reservoir

Astrakhan

CASPIAN SEA

MILES

0 50 100 150 200

North Caucasus Region

Between the Sea of Azov and the Black Sea in the west, the Caspian Sea in the east, and the lower Don and lower Volga in the north lies the North Caucasus Region, known for its farms, oil, and minerals. The northern part of the region is mostly a level plain, interrupted only by the low Stavropol' Plateau. Toward the south the land rises gradually at first, then suddenly, to the principal chain of the Caucasus. The Kuban' River drains the region westward to the Sea of Azov; the Kuma and Terek rivers drain east toward the Caspian Sea. The greater part of the North Caucasus Region is dry steppe, and forests are limited to the slopes of the Caucasus.

Russia first extended control over the North Caucasus plains during the eighteenth century, but conquest of the southern mountains was not completed until the 1860s. The native population remains largely in the mountains and the valleys of the Caucasus, concentrated in small villages. The Russian settlers, many of them Cossacks who were given land, built large villages and towns in the plain. The construction of a trunk railroad from Moscow and the lower Don Valley across the North Caucasus lowlands to the Caspian, in the latter part of the nineteenth century, finally tied the region firmly to the rest of European Russia.

The leading agricultural area of the North Caucasus Region is in the west, in the lowlands of the Kuban' River. Warm summers and the availability of water create an ideal setting for a variety of crops, ranging from hard wheat to oil seeds, sugar beets, tobacco, and rice. Extensive animal husbandry in the central steppes furnishes good beef as well as a large number of horses, while along the shore of the Black Sea, in the shelter of the Caucasus, tobacco and fruit are the main crops.

Coal in the north, an extension of the Donets coal deposits, oil and natural gas in the Caucasus foothills, and scattered hydroelectric installations provide energy. The leading industrial center is in the north, Rostov-na-Donu; here one of the Soviet Union's largest plants manufactures agricultural machinery. Oil refining, machine building, flour milling, and meat-packing are the characteristic industries of the cities of the plains, Krasnodar, Armavir, Nal'chik, and Groznyy. Novorossiysk, on the Black Sea, is a large producer of concrete and a seaport of more than local importance; Tuapse on the Black Sea and Makhachkala on the Caspian are terminals for pipelines from the North Caucasian oil fields.

The presence of hot springs in the Stavropol' Plateau led to the creation of popular spas. Along the sheltered shores of the Black Sea, the district and town of Sochi became one of the Soviet Union's most important seaside resorts in the 1930s.

The Rostov-na-Donu–Makhachkala railroad has served as the only rail link between the North Caucasus Region and the areas south of the Caucasus for over half a century. A second railroad, connecting Rostov-na-Donu and Armavir with Tuapse and the port of Batumi beyond the Caucasus, now provides another important access to the shores of the Black Sea in this region.

The Caucasus forms the southern boundary of the region, a true mountain barrier. Only trails traverse the range from north to south, and the sole highway link across the Caucasus crest is the Georgian Military Highway. Built in the mid-nineteenth century to connect the Trans-Caucasus and the North Caucasus plain, the Georgian Military Highway runs from Ordzhonikidze, the traditional gateway to the mountains, to Tbilisi, the capital of the Georgian Soviet Republic.

Centuries of isolation have preserved the complex structure of tribes, national groups, languages, and dialects in the Caucasus uplands down to our time. More than forty different languages are still spoken in these mountains.

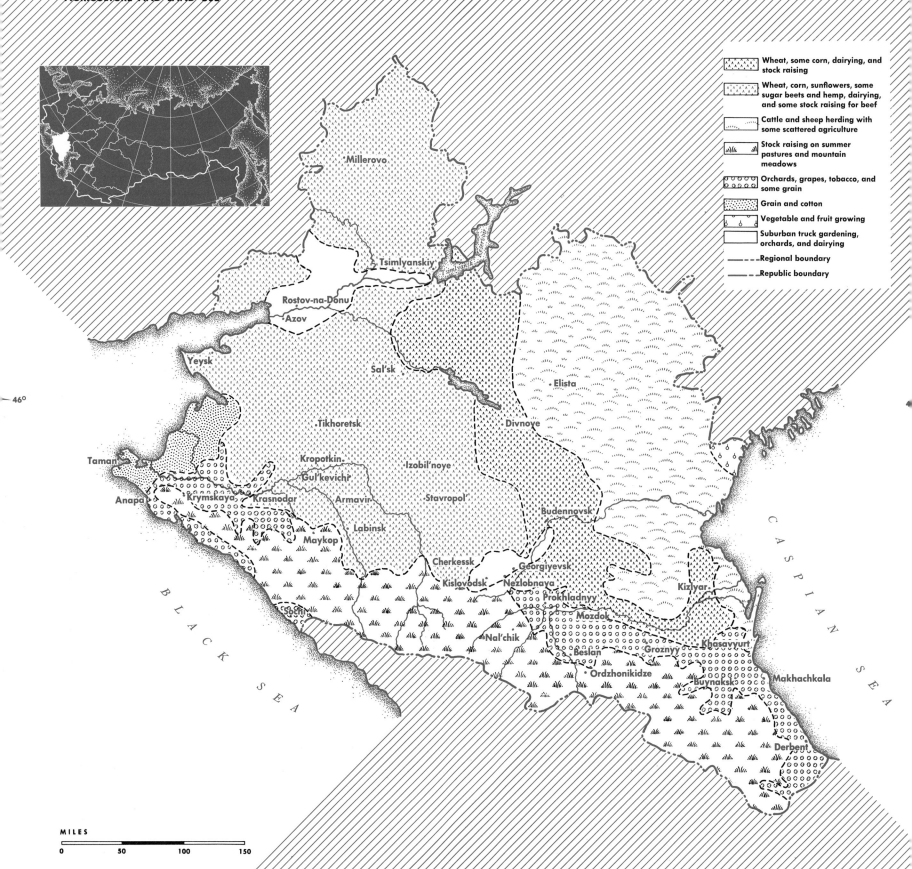

Wheat, some corn, dairying, and stock raising

Wheat, corn, sunflowers, some sugar beets and hemp, dairying, and some stock raising for beef

Cattle and sheep herding with some scattered agriculture

Stock raising on summer pastures and mountain meadows

Orchards, grapes, tobacco, and some grain

Grain and cotton

Vegetable and fruit growing

Suburban truck gardening, orchards, and dairying

Regional boundary

Republic boundary

Millerovo

Tsimlyanskiy

Tsimlyansk

Rostov-na-Donu

Azov

Yeysk

Sal'sk

Elista

Tikhoretsk

Divnoye

Taman'

Kropotkin

Izobil'noye

Gul'kevichi

Anapa

Krymskaya

Krasnodar

Armavir

Stavropol'

Budennovsk

Labinsk

Maykop

Cherkessk

Georgiyevsk

Kizlyar

Kislovodsk

Nezlobnaya

Prokhladnyy

Mozdok

Sochi

Nal'chik

Beslan

Groznyy

Khasavyurt

Ordzhonikidze

Makhachkala

Buynaksk

Derbent

BLACK SEA

CASPIAN SEA

MILES

0   50   100   150

Legend

- Coal
- Oil
- Oil refining
- Natural gas
- Iron ore
- M Manganese
- M Molybdenum
- Tungsten
- Lead, zinc, silver
- S Sulphur
- S Salt
- C Cement materials
- Building stone
- Oil pipeline
- Gas pipeline
- Gas pipeline under construction or planned
- Coal field
- Regional boundary
- Republic boundary

Kamensk-Shakhtinskiy

Koksovyy

Novoshakhtinsk

Shakhty

Taganrog

Rostov-na-Donu

DON

Tsimlyansk Reservoir

SEA OF AZOV

L. Manych-Gudilo

S

KUBAN'

Izobil'noye

Krasnodar

Armavir

Stavropol'

KUMA

Novorossiysk

Nevinnomyssk

Labinsk

Maykop

Neftegorsk

Tuapse

Sochi

TEREK

Malgobek

Tyrny-Auz

Gudermes

Groznyy

Alagir

Sadon

Ordzhonikidze

Makhachkala

Izberbash

Dagestanskiye Ogni

BLACK SEA

CASPIAN SEA

44°

46°

44°

MILES

0   50   100   150

INDUSTRY

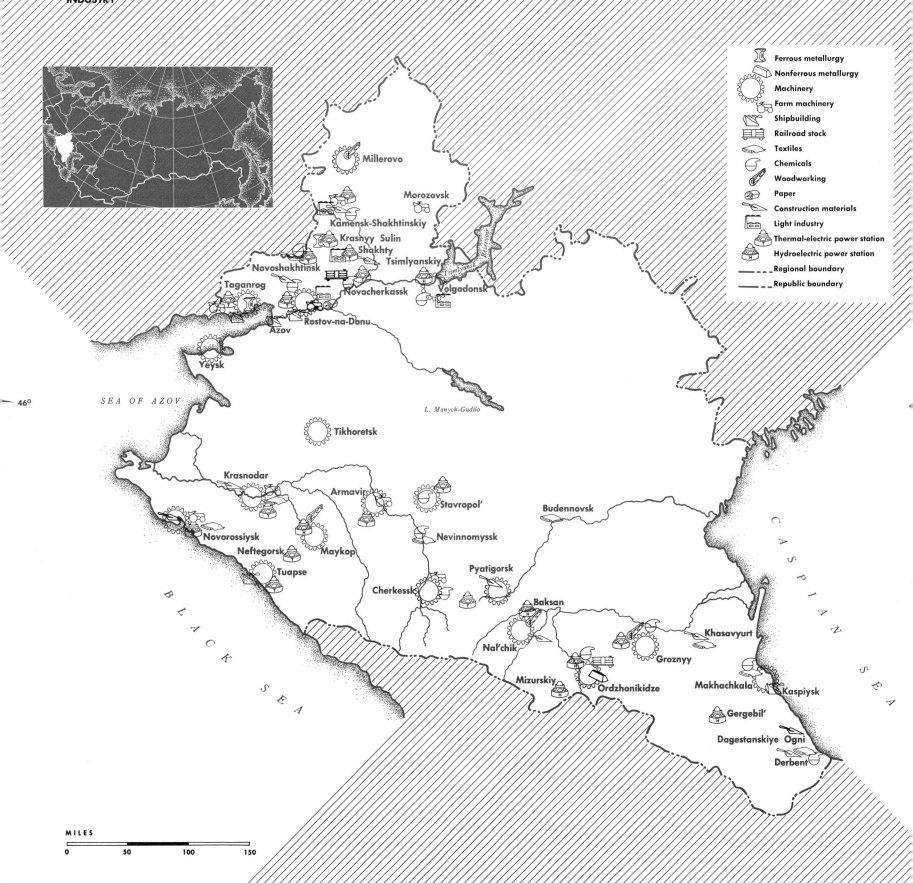

Legend:
- Ferrous metallurgy
- Nonferrous metallurgy
- Machinery
- Farm machinery
- Shipbuilding
- Railroad stock
- Textiles
- Chemicals
- Woodworking
- Paper
- Construction materials
- Light industry
- Thermal-electric power station
- Hydroelectric power station
- — · — Regional boundary
- — — — Republic boundary

Map labels:
- Millerovo
- Morozovsk
- Kamensk-Shakhtinskiy
- Krasnyy Sulin
- Shakhty
- Tsimlyanskiy
- Tsimlyansk Reservoir
- Novoshakhtinsk
- Taganrog
- Novocherkassk
- Volgodonsk
- Rostov-na-Donu
- Azov
- Yeysk
- SEA OF AZOV
- L. Manych-Gudilo
- Tikhoretsk
- Krasnodar
- Armavir
- Stavropol'
- Budennovsk
- Nevinnomyssk
- Novorossiysk
- Neftegorsk
- Maykop
- Pyatigorsk
- Tuapse
- Cherkessk
- Baksan
- Khasavyurt
- Nal'chik
- Groznyy
- Mizurskiy
- Ordzhonikidze
- Makhachkala
- Kaspiysk
- Gergebil'
- Dagestanskiye Ogni
- Derbent
- BLACK SEA
- CASPIAN SEA

MILES
0   50   100   150

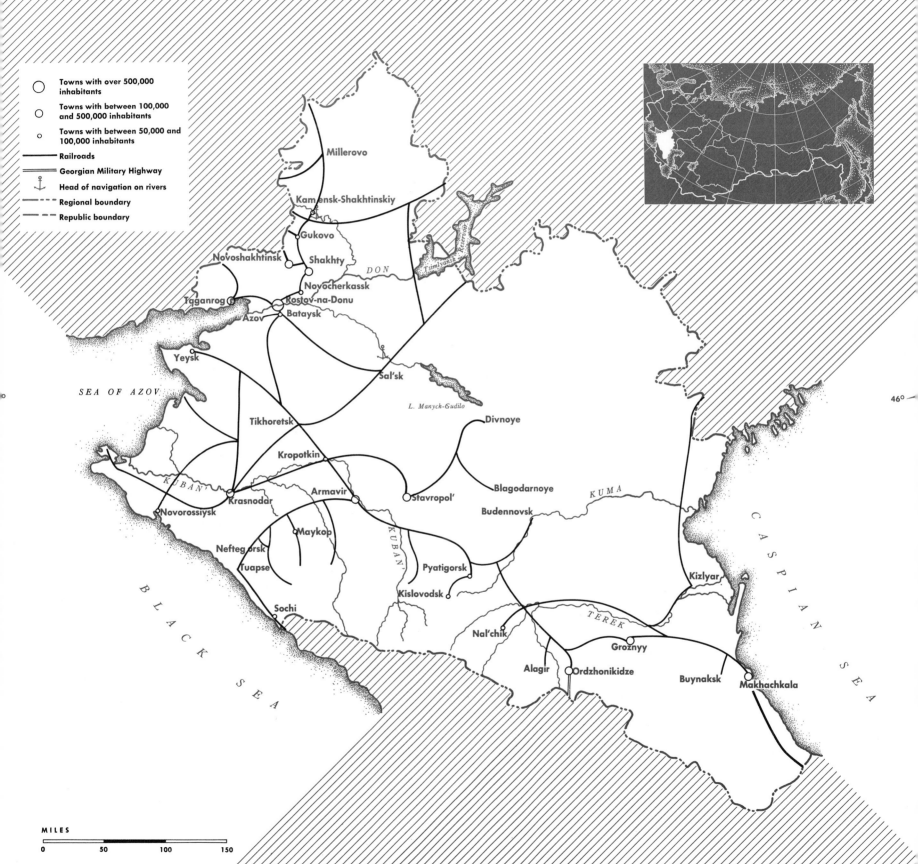

Towns with over 500,000 inhabitants

Towns with between 100,000 and 500,000 inhabitants

Towns with between 50,000 and 100,000 inhabitants

Railroads

Georgian Military Highway

Head of navigation on rivers

Regional boundary

Republic boundary

Millerovo

Kamensk-Shakhtinskiy

Gukovo

Novoshakhtinsk

Shakhty

Novocherkassk

DON

Tsimlyansk Reservoir

Taganrog

Rostov-na-Donu

Azov

Bataysk

Yeysk

Sal'sk

SEA OF AZOV

L. Manych-Gudilo

Divnoye

Tikhoretsk

Kropotkin

K U B A N'

Armavir

Stavropol'

Blagodarnoye

K U M A

Krasnodar

Budennovsk

Novorossiysk

Maykop

Neftegorsk

K U B A N'

Tuapse

Pyatigorsk

Kislovodsk

Kizlyar

Sochi

C A S P I A N   S E A

T E R E K

Nal'chik

Groznyy

B L A C K   S E A

Alagir

Ordzhonikidze

Buynaksk

Makhachkala

MILES

0   50   100   150

Trans-Caucasus Region

South of the main crest of the Caucasus lie the mountains, plains, and high plateaus of the Trans-Caucasus Region. Two lowlands—that of the Rioni River in the west, and that of the Kura and Araks rivers in the east—form the main farming areas. In the far south the Little Caucasus and other ranges connected with it form a mountainous zone that merges into the uplands of neighboring Turkey and Iran.

The far western Trans-Caucasus is warm and humid, with exceptionally mild winters. Eastward the climate rapidly changes to that of a semidesert, with large-scale variations of temperature, except in the tiny Lenkoran' district, sheltered by its mountain screen, near the Caspian Sea.

At one time this region was divided into kingdoms and principalities, Georgia and Armenia being the most impor-tant. But Islamic invasions from the south changed the ethnic and religious complexion, and until the Russian conquest early in the nineteenth century Turks and Persians ruled the entire region. Following the Communist revolution the Trans-Caucasus Region was divided into three Soviet Republics: Georgia in the west, Azerbaydzhan in the east, and Armenia in the south.

Farming in western Georgia, in the lowland of the Rioni River and on the warm lower slopes of the Caucasus over-looking the Black Sea, occupies a special place in the Soviet Union. This area, the "Soviet subtropics," is an important producer of tea, citrus fruit, and tung oil. Further east, in the warm, dry valleys of eastern Georgia, are the leading com-mercial vineyards of the Soviet Union. In the irrigated por-tions of the Kura-Araks lowland, cotton is the leading crop. Throughout the region the mountains serve as pasture for sheep and goats.

Oil is the single most important resource of the Trans-Caucasus; Baku and its district were from the 1860s to the 1940s the greatest oil fields of Russia. Even though Baku is now second to the Ural fields, production and refining of oil and the manufacturing of all kinds of machinery connected with it are the leading industries of the city of Baku. Oil is shipped out by rail or tanker to the European parts of the Soviet Union, by way of the Caspian and the Volga, or by pipeline to the export port of Batumi on the Black Sea. In addition to oil, manganese, copper, and barites are of more than local importance. Hydroelectric power is being devel-oped; the dam and reservoir on the Kura River, at Minge-chaur, is the largest of the region.

Tbilisi, Georgia's capital, and its suburbs and the city of Kutaisi are the only centers of metallurgy and machine building. Elsewhere food industries and textiles are the only branches of manufacturing. Tbilisi, on the upper Kura River, is also a major transportation center, connected by rail with Moscow, Baku on the Caspian, and neighboring Turkey.

Yerevan, the capital of the Armenian Soviet Republic, lies in the upper Araks Valley, dominated by the high, arid Armenian Plateau and by the majestic peaks of Ararat, a short distance away on Turkish territory.

Georgian, Armenian, and Azerbaydzhani (a language closely related to Turkish) are the main languages spoken in the Trans-Caucasus and the official languages of the schools in the three republics.

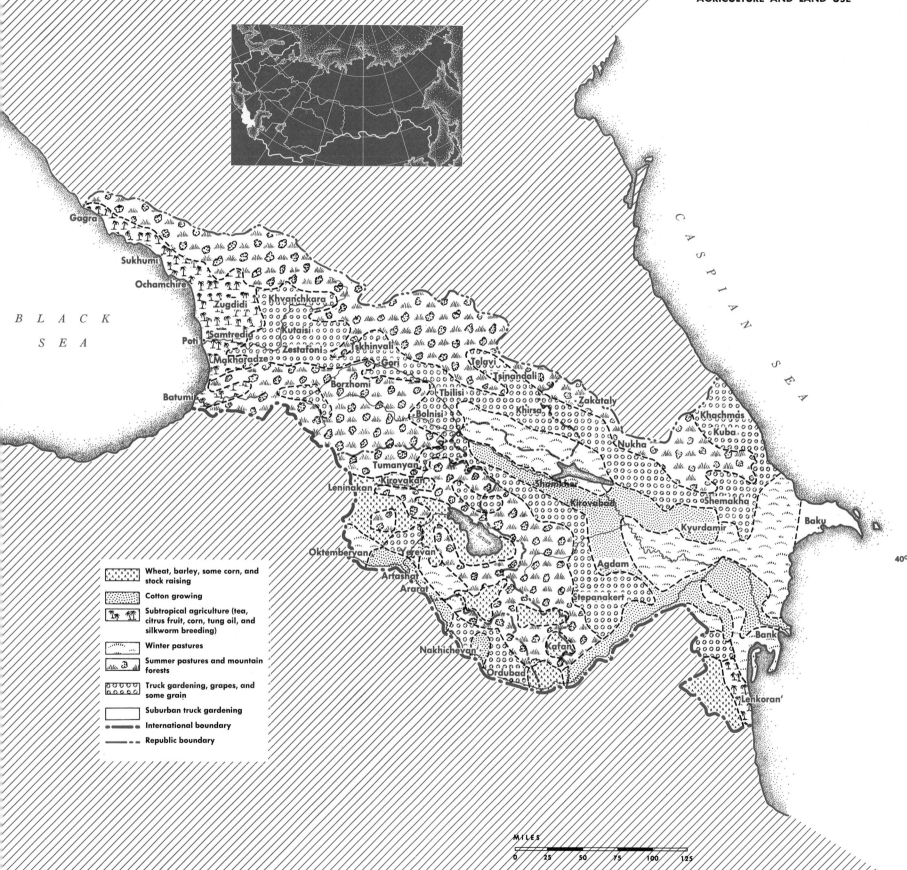

BLACK
SEA

CASPIAN SEA

Gagra

Sukhumi

Ochamchire

Zugdidi

Khvarichkara

Poti

Samtredia

Kutaisi

Zestafoni

Tskhinvali

Mkharadze

Telavi

Gori

Tsinandali

Borzhomi

Tbilisi

Zakataly

Batumi

Khirsa

Khachmas

Bolnisi

Nukha

Kuba

Tumanyan

Kirovakan

Shamkhor

Leninakan

Kirovabad

Shemakha

L. Sevan

Kyurdamir

Baku

Oktemberyan

Yerevan

Agdam

Artashat

Ararat

Stepanakert

Bank

Nakhichevan

Kafan

Ordubad

Lenkoran'

MILES

0 25 50 75 100 125

Legend

- Wheat, barley, some corn, and stock raising
- Cotton growing
- Subtropical agriculture (tea, citrus fruit, corn, tung oil, and silkworm breeding)
- Winter pastures
- Summer pastures and mountain forests
- Truck gardening, grapes, and some grain
- Suburban truck gardening
- International boundary
- Republic boundary

CASPIAN SEA

BLACK SEA

Tkvarcheli

RIONI

Kutaisi

Tkibuli

Chiatura

Kaspi

Borzhomi

Telavi

Tbilisi

Akhaltsikhe

Zakataly

Bolnisi

Mirzaani

Kuba

Akstafa

Alaverdi

Idzhevan

Kirovabad

Udzhary

Sumgait

Artik

Kirovakan

Zaglik

Naftalan

Anipemza

Dashkesan

Karadag

Baku

Yerevan

L. Sevan

KURA

Ararat

Nakhichevan'

Kadzharan

Kafan

ARAKS

Neftechala

Ordubad

Legend

- Coal
- Lignite
- Oil
- Oil refining
- Natural gas
- I Iron ore
- M Manganese
- Cobalt
- M Molybdenum
- AL Aluminum ore
- Tungsten
- C Copper
- CH Chromite
- Lead, zinc, silver
- B Barites
- S Sulphur and pyrites
- S Salt
- Graphite
- C Cement materials
- Building stone
- Oil pipeline
- Gas pipeline
- International boundary
- Republic boundary

MILES

0   25   50   75   100   125

B L A C K
S E A

C A S P I A N   S E A

Gagra
Sukhumi
Tkvarcheli
Ochamchire
Zugdidi
Poti
Chiatura
Kutaisi
Tskhinvali
Zestafoni
Kaspi
Samtredia
Gori
Telavi
Makharadze
Borzhomi
Tbilisi
Zakataly
Batumi
Akhaltsikhe
Khramges
Rustavi
Nukha
Alaverdi
Akstafa
Leninakan
Idzhevan
Mingechaur
Kirovakan
Kirovabad
Yevlakh
Sumgait
Artik
Gyumush
Dashkesan
Udzhary
Anipemza
Baku
Oktemberyan
Kamo
Karadag
Yerevan
Sabirabad
Artashat
Ararat
Stepanakert
Ali-Bayramly
Nakhichevan
Kafan
Sal'yany
Neftechala
Ordubad
Lenkoran'

Legend:

- Ferrous metallurgy
- Nonferrous metallurgy
- Machinery
- Farm machinery
- Shipbuilding
- Automobile industry
- Chemicals
- Textiles
- Cotton ginning
- Woodworking
- Paper
- Construction materials
- Light industry
- Thermal-electric power station
- Hydroelectric power station
- International boundary
- Republic boundary

MILES
0   25   50   75   100   125

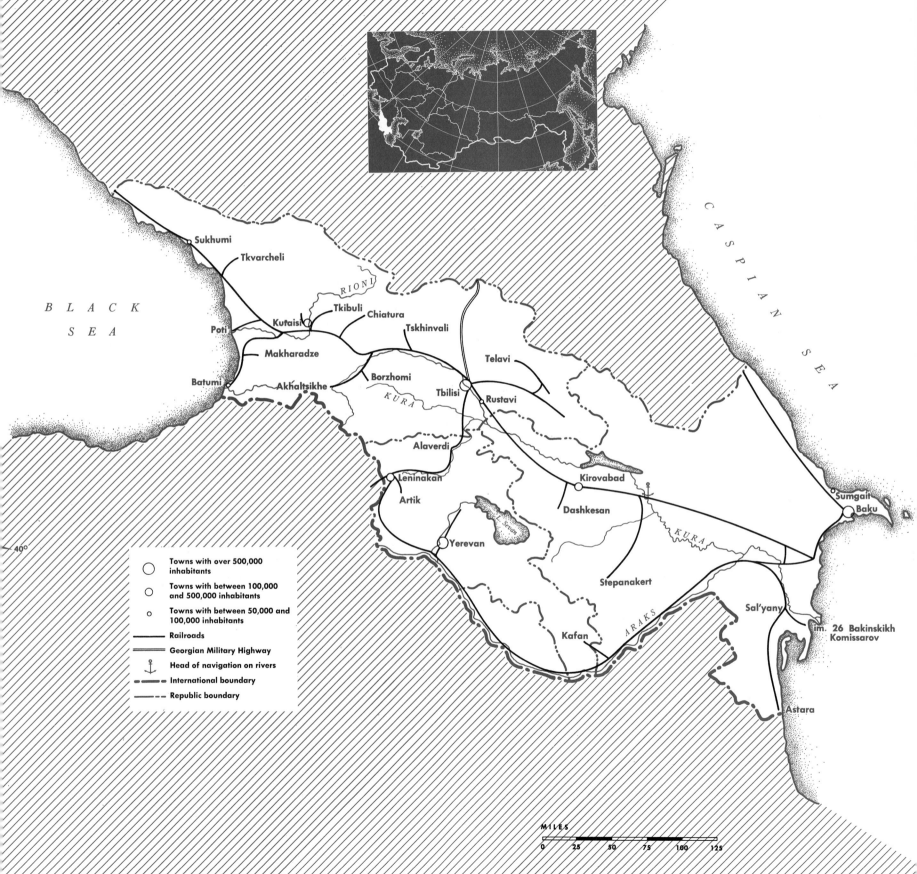

Legend:

○ Towns with over 500,000 inhabitants

○ Towns with between 100,000 and 500,000 inhabitants

○ Towns with between 50,000 and 100,000 inhabitants

— Railroads

Georgian Military Highway

⚓ Head of navigation on rivers

International boundary

Republic boundary

Map labels:

BLACK SEA

CASPIAN SEA

Sukhumi

Tkvarcheli

RIONI

Poti

Kutaisi

Tkibuli

Chiatura

Tskhinvali

Makharadze

Telavi

Batumi

Akhaltsikhe

Borzhomi

KURA

Tbilisi

Rustavi

Alaverdi

Kirovabad

Leninakan

Dashkesan

Artik

L. Sevan

Yerevan

Stepanakert

KURA

Sumgait

Baku

Sal'yany

im. 26 Bakinskikh Komissarov

Kafan

ARAKS

Astara

MILES

0   25   50   75   100   125

40°

46°

46°

Ural Region

The Ural Region represents the southern two-fifths of the Ural Mountains, a range that has long been considered the boundary between European Russia and Siberia. The Urals extend over 1,200 miles from north to south, from the tundra of the Arctic shore to the deserts north of the Caspian Sea. The sector of the Urals that has become a great industrial region was originally wooded, and charcoal from the Ural forests played an important part in the region's early industrial development.

The Urals represent a remnant of a mighty mountain system, heavily eroded and mineralized. Toward the west the range and its foothills slope gradually to the Volga, while in the east a noticeable escarpment separates the Urals from the Siberian plain. The northern part of the Ural Region is drained by the Pechora River to the northwest and by tributaries of the Ob' River to the northeast. The middle Urals' waterways are the Kama and Belaya rivers, tributaries of the Volga, in the west, and the Ob'-Irtysh drainage system in the east, while the southernmost Urals are drained by the Ural River to the Caspian Sea.

As a source of furs, the Urals were well known to medieval Russia. It was across this region that the Russian conquest of Siberia started in the sixteenth century, and ever since then all travel to Siberia has passed through the low Ural valleys. The presence of iron ore and charcoal gave rise to ferrous metallurgy in the seventeenth century, but Ural industry was on a small scale, and of low productivity, until after World War I. The choice of the Urals as a great industrial center of the future was motivated by their distance from the Soviet frontier and by the exceptional endowment of the region with metals and minerals. By the late 1950s the Urals had become the leading center of Soviet metallurgy.

The raw material base of Ural industry is unusual both in terms of the quantities of metals and minerals available and their variety. Iron, manganese, aluminum ore, potash, precious stones, and gold are all found in the Urals, and the discovery of oil on the western slopes led to the development of the largest group of Soviet oil fields known at present. Only high-quality coking coal is lacking, but coal from Kazakhstan makes up for most of this deficiency.

Ural industry was based at first on a close connection with coal from the Kuznetsk Basin of southwest Siberia, 1,200 miles distant by rail. During the 1920s and 1930s the greatest industrial growth took place on the eastern slopes and in the center of the Urals, where great mining centers like Magnitogorsk and vast cities of metallurgy and machines like Sverdlovsk and Chelyabinsk kept increasing their output throughout the early Five-Year Plans. The contribution of Ural industry to the Soviet war effort between 1941 and 1945 cannot be overestimated.

The oil fields of the western Urals, in the valleys of the Kama and the Belaya and of only local importance prior to World War II, became the leading producers of the Soviet Union in the 1950s. Crude oil and refined products are shipped from the western Ural Region to the Central Region, through the "Friendship" pipeline to Poland, East Germany, Czechoslovakia, and Hungary and as far east as Irkutsk, in eastern Siberia. Petrochemicals are now the most important product of industries in the western Urals, Perm' being the leading center of the area.

Five trunk railroads traverse the Urals in a west-east direction, connecting them with the Volga Valley, the Central Region, and Leningrad in the west, and Siberia and the Pacific in the east.

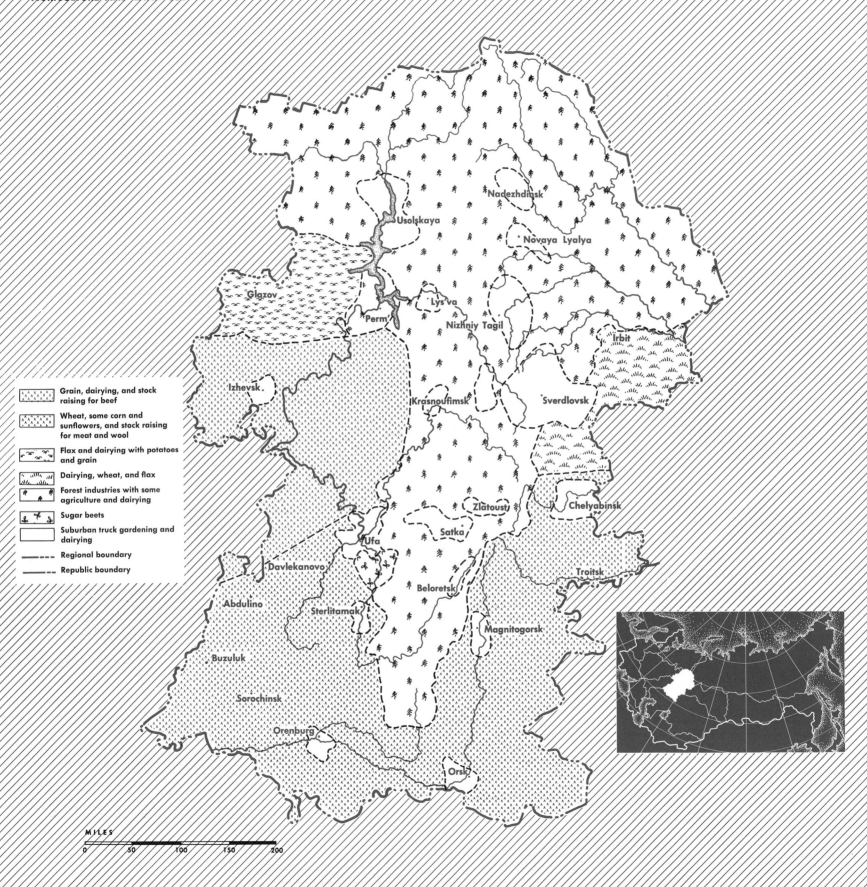

58°

Nadezhdinsk

Usolskaya

Novaya Lyalya

Glazov

Lys'va

Perm

Nizhniy Tagil

Irbit

Izhevsk.

Krasnoufimsk

Sverdlovsk

56°

Zlatoust

Chelyabinsk

Satka

Ufa

Davlekanovo

Beloretsk

Troitsk

Abdulino

Sterlitamak

Magnitogorsk

Buzuluk

Sorochinsk

Orenburg

Orsk

Legend:

- Grain, dairying, and stock raising for beef
- Wheat, some corn and sunflowers, and stock raising for meat and wool
- Flax and dairying with potatoes and grain
- Dairying, wheat, and flax
- Forest industries with some agriculture and dairying
- Sugar beets
- Suburban truck gardening and dairying
- — — — Regional boundary
- — ·· — Republic boundary

MILES

0   50   100   150   200

58°

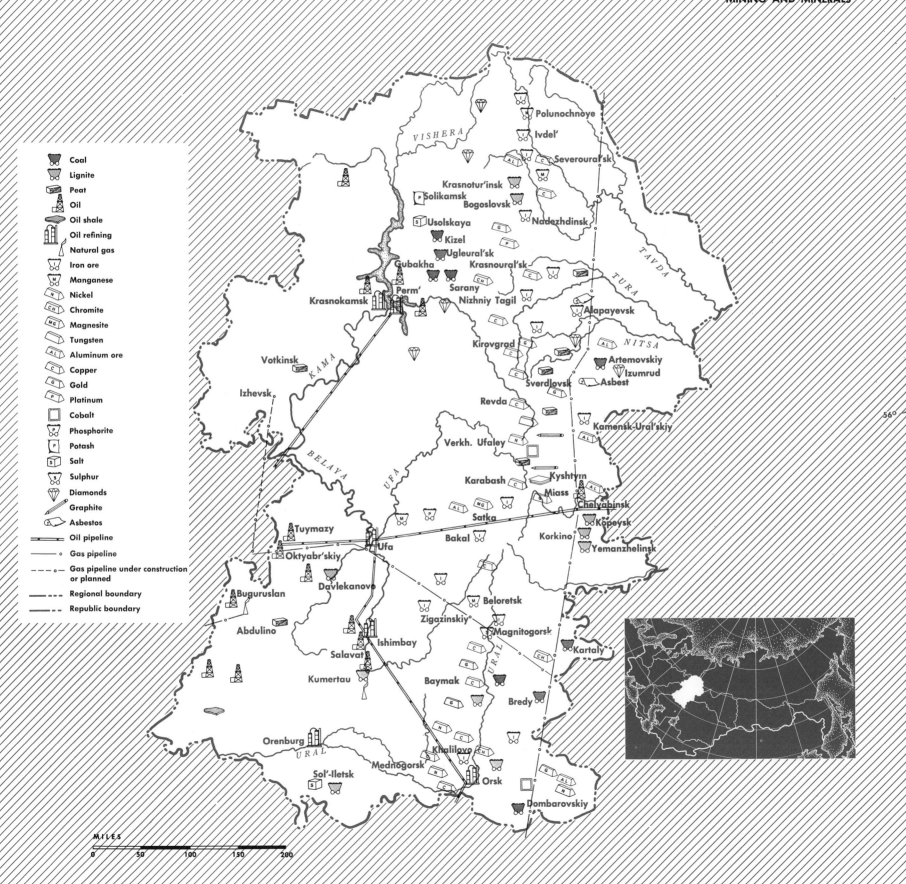

Legend

- Coal
- Lignite
- Peat
- Oil
- Oil shale
- Oil refining
- Natural gas
- Iron ore
- Manganese (M)
- Nickel (N)
- Chromite (CH)
- Magnesite (MG)
- Tungsten
- Aluminum ore (AL)
- Copper (C)
- Gold (G)
- Platinum (P)
- Cobalt
- Phosphorite (P)
- Potash (P)
- Salt (S)
- Sulphur (S)
- Diamonds
- Graphite
- Asbestos
- ▭▭ Oil pipeline
- —o Gas pipeline
- – – o Gas pipeline under construction or planned
- —·— Regional boundary
- —··— Republic boundary

Labels on map:

VISHERA, TAVDA, TURA, NITSA, KAMA, BELAYA, UFA, URAL

Polunochnoye, Ivdel', Severoural'sk, Krasnotur'insk, Solikamsk, Bogoslovsk, Usolskaya, Kizel, Nadezhdinsk, Ugleural'sk, Krasnoural'sk, Gubakha, Sarany, Krasnokamsk, Perm', Nizhniy Tagil, Alapayevsk, Kirovgrad, Artemovskiy, Votkinsk, Izumrud, Sverdlovsk, Asbest, Izhevsk, Revda, Kamensk-Ural'skiy, Verkh. Ufaley, Kyshtym, Karabash, Miass, Chelyabinsk, Satka, Bakal, Kopeysk, Tuymazy, Korkino, Ufa, Yemanzhelinsk, Oktyabr'skiy, Davlekanovo, Buguruslan, Beloretsk, Abdulino, Zigazinskiy, Ishimbay, Magnitogorsk, Salavat, Kartaly, Kumertau, Baymak, Bredy, Orenburg, Khalilovo, Mednogorsk, Sol'-Iletsk, Orsk, Dombarovskiy

MILES
0   50   100   150   200

Legend:

- Ferrous metallurgy
- Nonferrous metallurgy
- Machinery
- Farm machinery
- Shipbuilding
- Railroad stock
- Automobile industry
- Chemicals
- Textiles
- Woodworking
- Paper
- Construction materials
- Light industry
- Thermal-electric power station
- Hydroelectric power station
- Atomic power station
- Regional boundary
- Republic boundary

58°

Krasnovishersk
Ivdel'
Severoural'sk
Krasnotur'insk
Borovsk
Solikamsk
Bogoslovsk
Usolskaya
Nadezhdinsk
Sos'va
Maykop
Kizel
Kudymkar
Novaya Lyalya
Chermoz
Gubakha
Krasnoural'sk
Dobryanka
Kushva
Turinsk
Krasnokamsk
Chusovoy
Nizhnyaya Salda
Glazov
Perm'
Nizhniy Tagil
Tavda
Lys'va
Alapayevsk
Irbit
Kirovgrad
Kungur
Pervoural'sk
Artemovskiy
Troitskiy
Uva
Nizh. Sergi
Sukhoy Log
Votkinsk
Sverdlovsk
Izhevsk
Revda
Mozhga
Sarapul
Krasnoufimsk
Beloyarsk
Polevskoy
Kamensk-Ural'skiy
Verkh. Ufaley
Kasli
Pavlovka
Kyshtym
Karabash
Krasnousol'skiy
Zlatoust
Kartaly
Asha
Satka
Chelyabinsk
Ufa
Ust'-Katav
Chebarkul'
Tuymazy
Miass
Tirlyanskiy
Beloretsk
Troitsk
Belebey
Sterlitamak
Ishimbay
Magnitogorsk
Bugurulsan
Kartaly
Buzuluk
Baymak
Orenburg
Saraktash
Mednogorsk
Orsk
Sol'-Iletsk
Novotroitsk

56°

MILES
0   50   100   150   200

58°

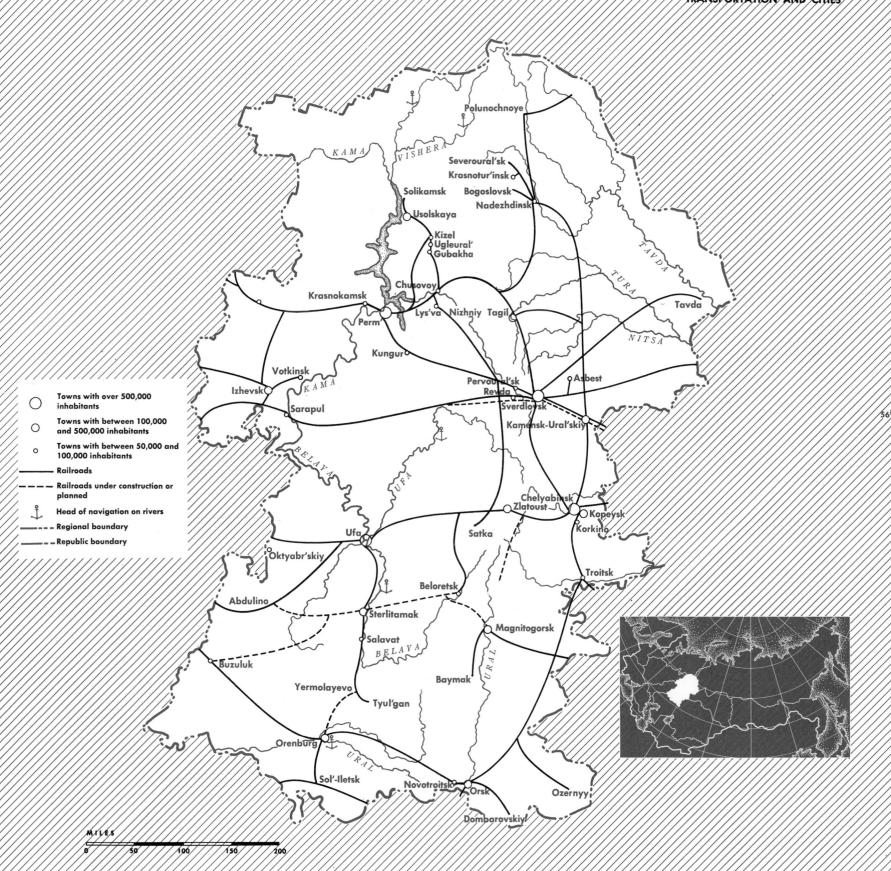

KAMA

VISHERA

Polunochnoye

Severoural'sk

Krasnotur'insk

Bogoslovsk

Nadezhdinsk

Solikamsk

Usolskaya

Kizel
Ugleural'
Gubakha

TAVDA

Chusovoy

Krasnokamsk

Lys'va Nizhniy Tagil

Tavda

Perm

TURA

Kungur

NITSA

Votkinsk

Pervoural'sk
Revda

Asbest

Izhevsk

KAMA

Sverdlovsk

Sarapul

Kamensk-Ural'skiy

Towns with over 500,000
inhabitants

Towns with between 100,000
and 500,000 inhabitants

Towns with between 50,000 and
100,000 inhabitants

Railroads

Railroads under construction or
planned

Head of navigation on rivers

Regional boundary

Republic boundary

BELAYA

UFA

Chelyabinsk
Zlatoust

Kopeysk

Korkino

Ufa

Satka

Oktyabr'skiy

Troitsk

Beloretsk

Abdulino

Sterlitamak

Magnitogorsk

Salavat

Buzuluk

BELAYA

Yermolayevo

Baymak

URAL

Tyul'gan

Orenburg

Sol'-Iletsk

URAL

Novotroitsk Orsk

Ozernyy

Dombarovskiy

MILES

0   50   100   150   200

West Siberian Region

East of the Urals lies the wide, nearly level plain of Western Siberia, drained northward by the Ob' and Irtysh rivers and their tributaries. This is the agricultural heart of the region. In the southeast, the land rises to the Altai Range, dissected by streams tributary to the Ob'. This area, richly endowed with fuels and significant deposits of metals, is the region's industrial heart. Toward the north, Western Siberia touches on the marshy, thinly populated forests that are part of the Far North.

This is the region where the Russians first entered Siberia in the sixteenth century, when small bands of traders established outposts at river crossings and, using rivers and portages, launched the adventure that was to take the Russians across Siberia to the Pacific in less than a century. Tyumen', almost within sight of the Urals, was the first Russian permanent settlement in Siberia, and symbolically also the terminus of the first Trans-Ural railroad that connected it with European Russia in the late nineteenth century. It was from Tyumen', too, that construction of the Trans-Siberian railroad started in 1891, and as the railroad advanced, it was followed by waves of settlers from the thickly populated lands of European Russia.

The plains of Western Siberia have been ploughed for nearly three-quarters of a century, and are among the best producers of grain and livestock in the Soviet Union. Wheat is the principal grain, followed by rye and oats. Sugar beets (along the southern and southwestern margins), flax, and potatoes are the industrial crops. Most of the cattle are dairy cattle. Western Siberia has been a surplus producer of milk, cheese, and butter from the beginnings of European settlement. Since World War II there has been a sustained effort to extend the crop acreage toward the dry margins, an enterprise as yet uncertain in outcome.

The hilly and mountainous southeastern area of the West Siberian Region contains the largest single deposit of coal in the Soviet Union, the Kuznetsk Basin. These deposits are located in the valley of the Tom', a tributary of the Ob'. They have been mined since the turn of the century. Large-scale exploitation of the Kuznetsk Basin, however, dates from the late 1920s, when the Ural-Kuznetsk "kombinat" came into existence. Kuznetsk coal was then shipped in large quantities to the Ural blast furnaces, while Ural iron ore formed the return freight and became the base for the building of a complex of ferrous metallurgy in the Kuznetsk Basin in Kemerovo, Novokuznetsk, and other cities. The intensity of Ural-Kuznetsk traffic is considerably less now, due to the use of local ores in the Kuznetsk Basin and to the increased use of coal from Kazakhstan in the Ural industries. Besides iron and steel, machinery and chemicals are the important heavy industries of the Kuznetsk Basin.

Novosibirsk is the largest city and leading transportation center of the West Siberian Region, and a strong second in industry to the Kuznetsk Basin. Located at the intersection of the Ob' River and the main line of the Trans-Siberian railroad, Novosibirsk is a natural focus of routes. Since the early 1930s it is also the Siberian terminal of the Turk-Sib railroad, linking it with Soviet Central Asia.

The second west-east trunk railroad of the region, the South Siberian railroad, connects the southern Urals with West Siberia and extends to the Kuznetsk Basin. Barnaul, at the junction of the South Siberian and Turk-Sib railroads, is a city of varied industries; Rubtsovsk, in the southernmost part of the region, is the principal producer of farm machinery for West Siberia.

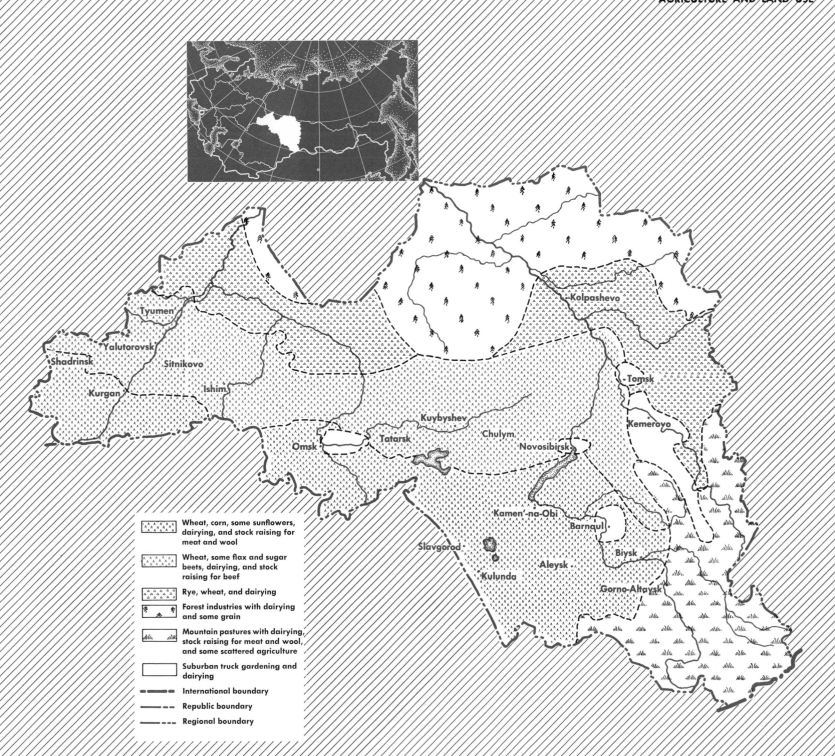

Wheat, corn, some sunflowers, dairying, and stock raising for meat and wool

Wheat, some flax and sugar beets, dairying, and stock raising for beef

Rye, wheat, and dairying

Forest industries with dairying and some grain

Mountain pastures with dairying, stock raising for meat and wool, and some scattered agriculture

Suburban truck gardening and dairying

International boundary

Republic boundary

Regional boundary

80°

Tyumen'
Yalutorovsk
Shadrinsk
Sitnikovo
Kurgan
Ishim
Kolpashevo
Tomsk
Kuybyshev
Kemerovo
Chulym
Omsk
Tatarsk
Novosibirsk
Kamen'-na-Obi
Barnaul
Slavgorod
Biysk
Aleysk
Kulunda
Gorno-Altaysk

55°
80°

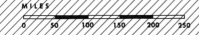

MILES
0   50   100   150   200   250

West Siberian Region

MINING AND MINERALS

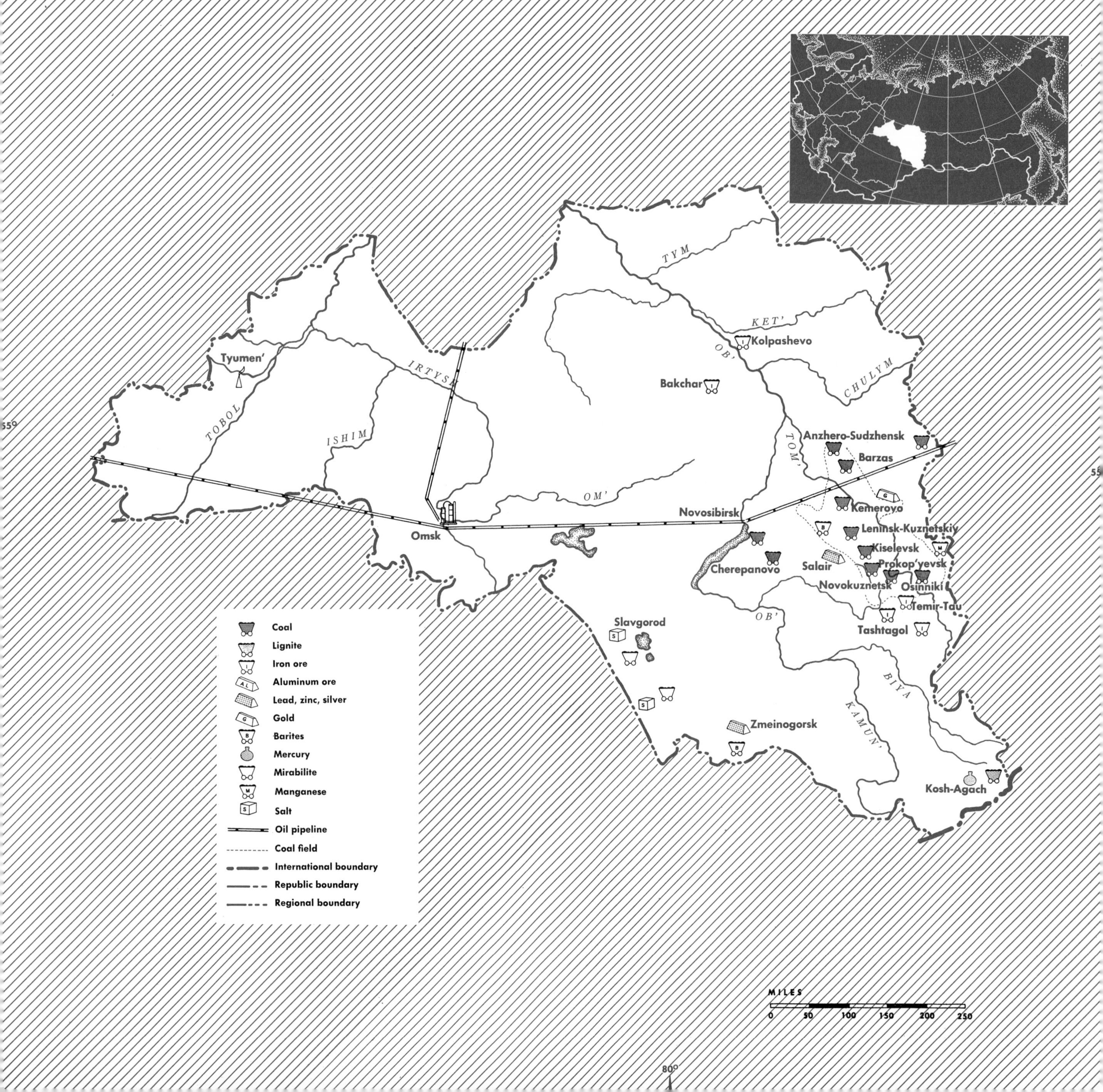
80°
55°
TYM
KET'
OB'
CHULYM
IRTYSH
TOBOL
ISHIM
OM'
TOM'
BIYA
KAMUN'
Tyumen'
Kolpashevo
Bakchar
Anzhero-Sudzhensk
Barzas
Kemerovo
Novosibirsk
Omsk
Leninsk-Kuznetskiy
Kiselevsk
Prokop'yevsk
Cherepanovo
Salair
Novokuznetsk
Osinniki
Temir-Tau
Tashtagol
Slavgorod
Zmeinogorsk
Kosh-Agach
Coal
Lignite
Iron ore
Aluminum ore
Lead, zinc, silver
Gold
Barites
Mercury
Mirabilite
Manganese
Salt
Oil pipeline
Coal field
International boundary
Republic boundary
Regional boundary
MILES
0
50
100
150
200
250

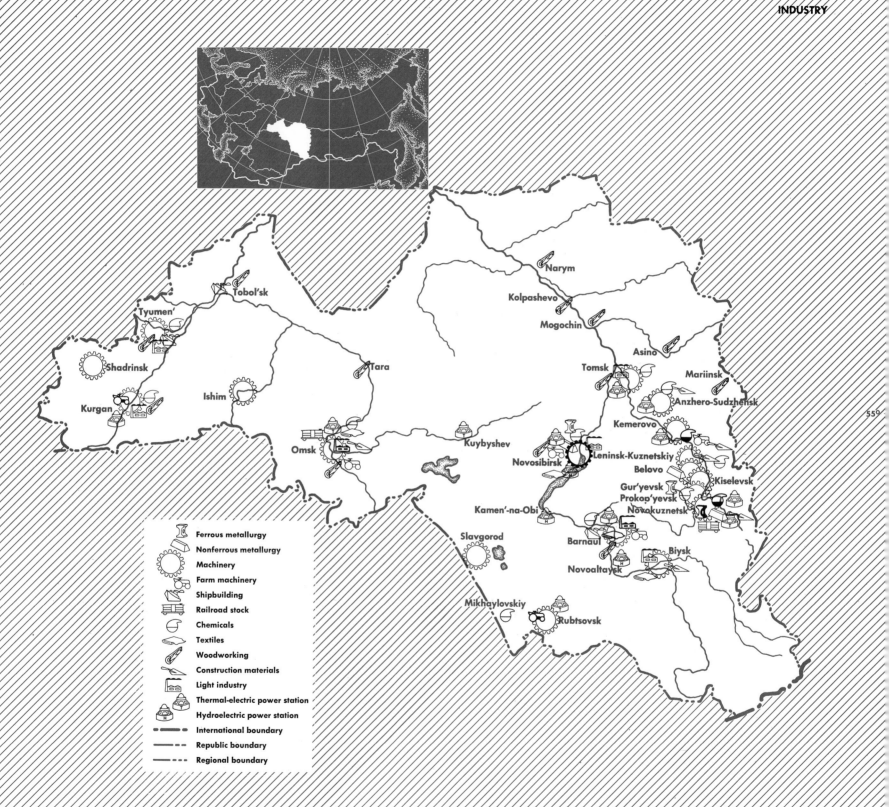

80°

Narym

Kolpashevo

Mogochin

Asino

Tobol'sk

Tyumen'

Tomsk

Mariinsk

Anzhero-Sudzhensk

Shadrinsk

Tara

Kemerovo

Kurgan

Ishim

Kuybyshev

Leninsk-Kuznetskiy

Novosibirsk

Belovo

Omsk

Kiselevsk

Gur'yevsk

Prokop'yevsk

Kamen'-na-Obi

Novokuznetsk

Slavgorod

Barnaul

Biysk

Novoaltaysk

Mikhaylovskiy

Rubtsovsk

559

	Ferrous metallurgy
	Nonferrous metallurgy
	Machinery
	Farm machinery
	Shipbuilding
	Railroad stock
	Chemicals
	Textiles
	Woodworking
	Construction materials
	Light industry
	Thermal-electric power station
	Hydroelectric power station
	International boundary
	Republic boundary
	Regional boundary

80°

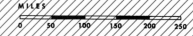

MILES
0   50   100   150   200   250

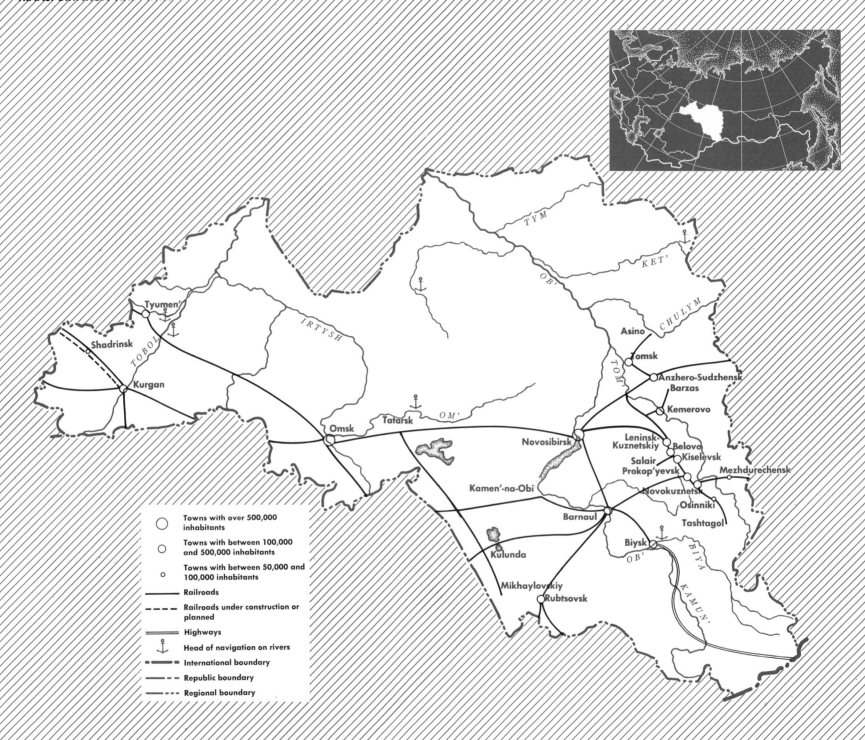

TYM

KET'

CHULYM

OB'

IRTYSH

TOBOL

Tyumen'

Shadrinsk

Kurgan

Asino

Tomsk

Anzhero-Sudzhensk
Barzas

TOM'

Kemerovo

Omsk

Tatarsk

OM'

Novosibirsk

Leninsk-
Kuznetskiy

Belovo
Salair
Prokop'yevsk
Kiselevsk

Mezhdurechensk

Kamen'-na-Obi

Novokuznetsk

Osinniki

Barnaul

Tashtagol

Kulunda

Biysk

OB'

BIYA

KAMUN'

Mikhaylovskiy
Rubtsovsk

Towns with over 500,000
inhabitants

Towns with between 100,000
and 500,000 inhabitants

Towns with between 50,000 and
100,000 inhabitants

Railroads

Railroads under construction or
planned

Highways

Head of navigation on rivers

International boundary

Republic boundary

Regional boundary

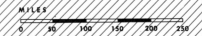

MILES

0   50   100   150   200   250

East Siberian Region

The mountains, plateaus, and intermontane basins of East Siberia form the central portion of the long narrow band of settlement in Siberia that follows the Trans-Siberian railroad to the Pacific coast. Lake Baykal, the largest lake of Siberia and the deepest lake in the world, forms the center of the region. To the west the great arc of the Sayan Mountains occupies much of the land; to the east the Yablonovyy Mountains and their adjacent basins extend to the region's eastern boundary. Most of the region is covered with forests of pine and larch; areas of grasslands occupy the intermontane basins. The climate is harsh, and there are sizable areas of permanently frozen subsoil in the East Siberian Region.

Agriculture is carried on only in scattered areas, oats being the primary crop. Animal husbandry, the raising of cattle, sheep, and horses, is more rewarding than crops in this region. Food industries are limited to meat-packing and the processing of dairy products.

Mining has long been the principal industry of East Siberia. There is a wide range of metals and minerals, such as gold, tin, graphite, mica, and zinc. West of Lake Baykal lie the main coal deposits, the coal fields of Cheremkhovo on the Angara River and of Minusinsk in the upper valley of the Yenisey. The Angara, a tributary of the Yenisey that drains Lake Baykal, is one of the Soviet rivers best adapted for the development of hydroelectric power: the Bratsk hydroelectric plant on the Angara is the largest in the world.

All of the cities and industries of the East Siberian Region lie along the Trans-Siberian railroad. Irkutsk, the largest city of the region, is one of the oldest Russian settlements in Siberia, located on the Angara River a short distance from Lake Baykal. Krasnoyarsk, where the Trans-Siberian railroad crosses the Yenisey River, is a center of machine industries. Ulan-Ude, east of Lake Baykal, and Chita specialize in railroad rolling stock and food industries.

The Trans-Siberian railroad has been the lifeline of East Siberia since the first years of the twentieth century, its only link with European Russia and the Far East. Increasing Soviet interest in Outer Mongolia led, first, to the building of a rail spur from Ulan-Ude to the Soviet-Mongol boundary, later to the Mongol capital of Ulan Bator, and, in 1954, to the completion of a railroad that links East Siberia and Ulan Bator with Peking and all of North China across Outer Mongolia. Besides providing all-weather mass transportation for Outer Mongolia, this new line shortens the rail connections between Moscow and Peking by over 600 miles.

The Tuva district, in the southwestern part of East Siberia, has been a Russian sphere of influence since the turn of the century, but was not officially incorporated in the Soviet Union until 1944. Its best-known resource is asbestos.

Lake Baykal, in the center of East Siberia, is important for fisheries and exerts a moderating influence on the climate of the areas adjacent to its shores.

Although Russians form the vast majority of the population in East Siberia, two non-Russian groups appear in large enough numbers to be given territorial recognition through the formation of the Autonomous Regions. They are the Buryat-Mongols and the people of the Tuva district.

Grain, dairying, and stock raising for beef

Stock raising for meat and wool, and some grain

Tayga: reindeer herding, hunting, and trapping

Forest industries with some agriculture along the river valleys

Forest industries and stock raising for meat and wool in mountain regions

Suburban truck gardening

International boundary

Regional boundary

105°

55°

Bogotol
Achinsk
Krasnoyarsk

Abakan
Minusinsk

Kyzyl

Tulun

Nizhne-Angarsk

Baykal

Irkutsk

Ulan-Ude

Ganzurino

Chita

Nerchinsk

Borzya

105°

MILES
0   100   200   300

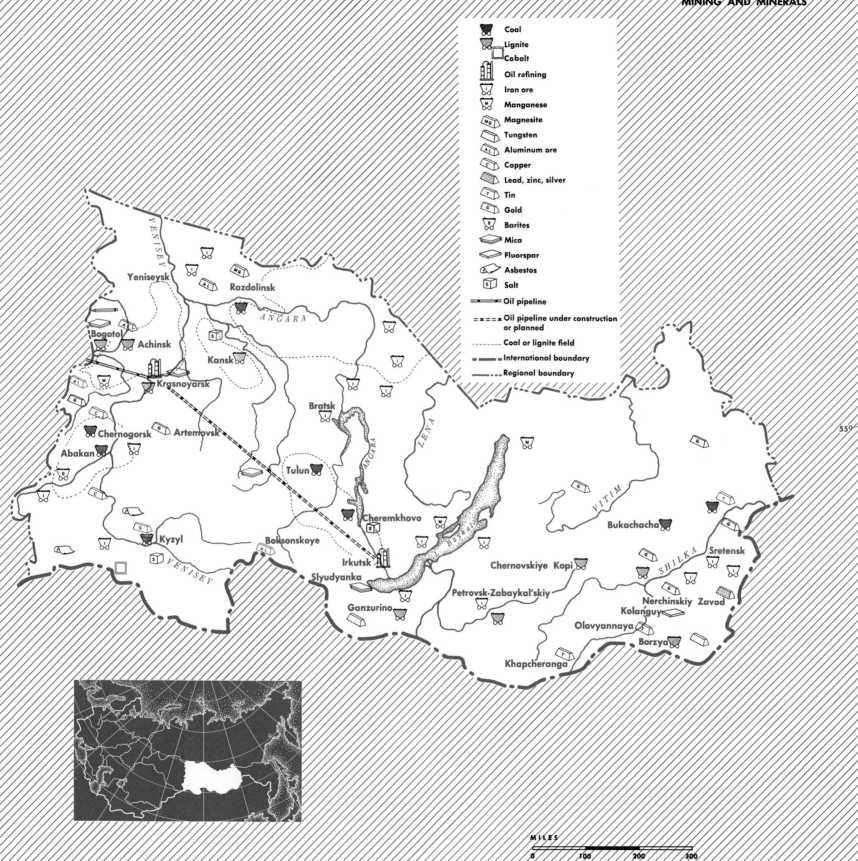

Legend

- Coal
- Lignite
- Cobalt
- Oil refining
- Iron ore
- Manganese
- Magnesite
- Tungsten
- Aluminum ore
- Copper
- Lead, zinc, silver
- Tin
- Gold
- Barites
- Mica
- Fluorspar
- Asbestos
- Salt
- Oil pipeline
- Oil pipeline under construction or planned
- Coal or lignite field
- International boundary
- Regional boundary

Place names:

Yeniseysk
Razdolinsk
ANGARA
Bogotol
Achinsk
Kansk
Krasnoyarsk
Bratsk
Chernogorsk
Artemovsk
Abakan
Tulun
Cheremkhovo
Kyzyl
Boksonskoye
Irkutsk
Slyudyanka
Ganzurino
Petrovsk-Zabaykal'skiy
Chernovskiye Kopi
Bukachacha
Sretensk
Nerchinskiy Zavod
Kolanguy
Olovyannaya
Borzya
Khapcheranga
YENISEY
LENA
VITIM
SHILKA
BAYKAL

MILES
0   100   200   300

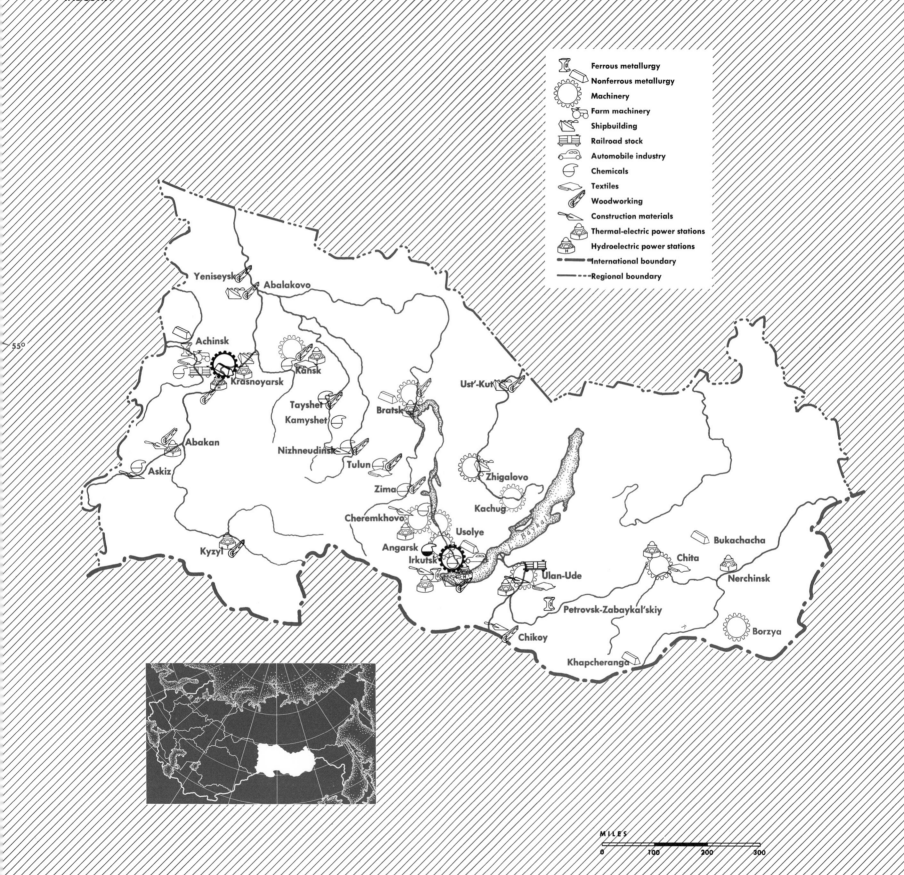

Ferrous metallurgy
Nonferrous metallurgy
Machinery
Farm machinery
Shipbuilding
Railroad stock
Automobile industry
Chemicals
Textiles
Woodworking
Construction materials
Thermal-electric power stations
Hydroelectric power stations
International boundary
Regional boundary

Yeniseysk
Abalakovo
Achinsk
Krasnoyarsk
Kansk
Taysher
Kamyshet
Bratsk
Ust'-Kut
Abakan
Nizhneudinsk
Askiz
Tulun
Zhigalovo
Zima
Kachug
Cheremkhovo
Usolye
Kyzyl
Angarsk
Irkutsk
Ulan-Ude
Bukachacha
Chita
Nerchinsk
Petrovsk-Zabaykal'skiy
Borzya
Chikoy
Khapcheranga

Baykal

MILES
0   100   200   300

Towns with between 100,000 and 500,000 inhabitants

Towns with between 50,000 and 100,000 inhabitants

Railroads

Railroads under construction or planned

Highways

Head of navigation on rivers

International boundary

Regional boundary

105°

YENISEY

ANGARA

Maklakovo
Abalakovo

Achinsk

Krasnoyarsk

Kansk

Tayshet

Bratsk

Ust'-Kut

LENA

55°

Chernogorsk

Abakan

VITIM

Zima

Cheremkhovo

Bukachacha

SHILKA

Angarsk

ANGARA

Baykal

Irkutsk

Sretensk

Kyzyl

YENISEY

Ulan-Ude

Chita

Ganzurino

Borzya

To Ulan-Bator
Peking

To Harbin

MILES

0   100   200   300

Far Eastern Region

The Far Eastern Region is the Soviet gateway to the Pacific, China, Japan, and Korea. Since the seventeenth century, when Russia first reached the shores of the Pacific and gained a foothold in this region, it has been the spearhead of Russian advance toward the Far East. After the first Russian settlement was established in 1658 at Okhotsk, on the Sea of Okhotsk which is part of the Pacific Ocean, Russian pressure on China resulted in the treaty of 1689 at Nerchinsk. This, the first treaty concluded between China and a European nation, ceded to the Russians land east of Lake Baykal, including the upper reaches of the Amur River. In 1858 a second treaty extended Russian control to all of the left bank of the middle Amur, the entire lower Amur Valley, and the land between the lower Amur and the Pacific Ocean. After several boundary changes the island of Sakhalin and the Kuril Islands, between Sakhalin and the Kamchatka Peninsula, are now in Soviet hands, establishing Soviet control over the entire northeast coast of Asia from Korea to Alaska, a distance of over 3,000 miles.

The greatest part of the Far Eastern Region is mountainous. European settlements, except for mining outposts, compose a Y-shaped area, formed by the middle and lower valley of the Amur River and the valley of the Ussuri River, as far as the city of Vladivostok on the Pacific. Evergreen forests cover most of the region, but in its southern parts trees, bushes, and flowering plants are those of Monsoon Asia, of Korea, Manchuria, and Japan.

Agriculture is limited by the mountainous character of the region to scattered areas in river valleys. The range of crops is surprisingly wide in the few farming areas: soybeans, sugar beets, and corn in addition to wheat, oats, and hay. More important in the economy of the region than farming are fishing, hunting, and trapping. The waters of the Pacific, as well as the rivers, are rich in marine life: sturgeon, salmon, Pacific cod, and crabs abound. Seal are hunted offshore, and there is some whaling. The fur-bearing animals of the forests of the Far East include not only ermine, silver fox, and sable but also, in the southern parts, the Ussuri tiger.

The mineral deposits of the region are notable for their abundance and variety, although exploitation is still on a relatively limited scale. Coal in the northwestern and southern areas and oil and coal from the island of Sakhalin are the principal sources of fuel. Metals and minerals range from gold to iron ore, tin, lead, and zinc.

Settlements follow closely the main artery of the region, the Trans-Siberian railroad. After the loss of the original Trans-Siberian line, which crossed Manchuria on its way to the Pacific, at the close of the Russo-Japanese War in 1905, a new track was laid which follows the Amur to its confluence with the Ussuri and thence continues south to its terminus, the port of Vladivostok. Since World War I additional railroads were built to connect new settlements with the Trans-Siberian trunk line, as well as several major highways serving remote mining areas.

Industrial development in the Soviet Far East was strongly supported by the government following World War I, in order to create a nearly independent supply base for Soviet forces, in the event of another Russo-Japanese war. Thus heavy and light industries, though on a modest scale, are found in the region: metallurgy, machine building and shipbuilding, smelting and refining, and textile, clothing, and food industries.

Vladivostok, long the leading Soviet port on the Pacific, now shares that role with the neighboring port of Nakhodka. Khabarovsk, at the junction of the Amur and Ussuri rivers, is the region's most important center for rail and air transport. Its industries include farm machinery, sawmills, and a shipyard. Komsomol'sk, on the lower Amur, is the most diversified industrial city of the Soviet Far East; it is served by the Amur River, and by railroads leading to Khabarovsk and to the Pacific port of Sovetskaya Gavan'.

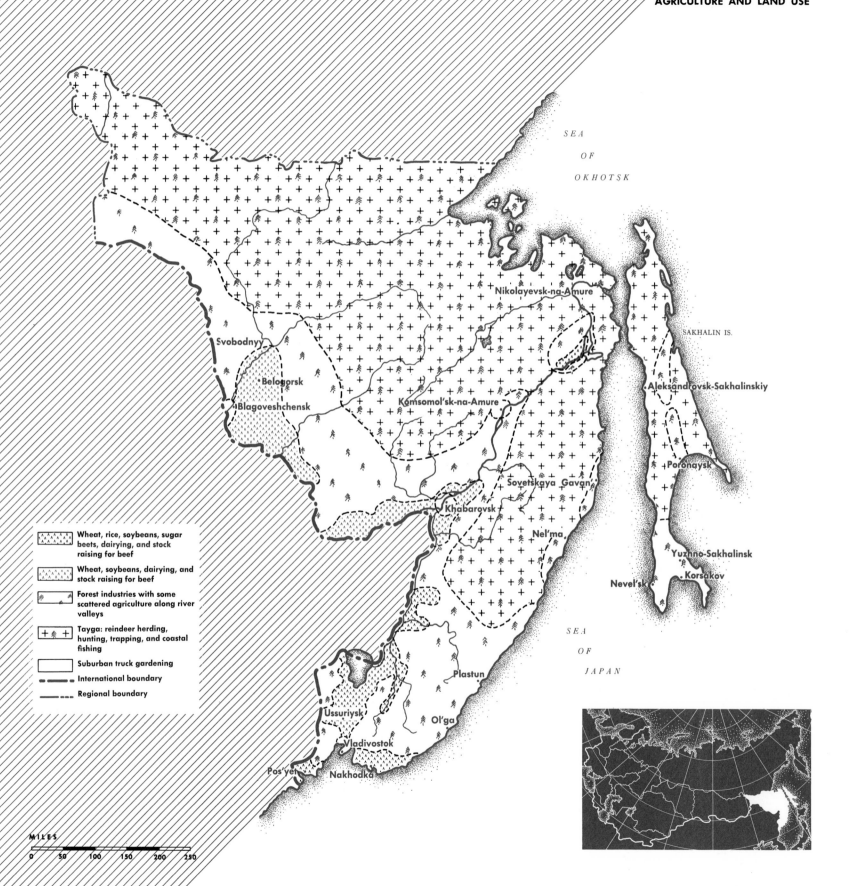

130°

SEA
OF
OKHOTSK

Nikolayevsk-na-Amure

SAKHALIN IS.

Svobodnyy

Belogorsk

Blagoveshchensk

Komsomol'sk-na-Amure

Aleksandrovsk-Sakhalinskiy

50°

Poronaysk

Sovetskaya Gavan'

Khabarovsk

Nel'ma

Yuzhno-Sakhalinsk

Korsakov

Nevel'sk

SEA
OF
JAPAN

Plastun

Ussuriysk

Ol'ga

Vladivostok

Pos'yet   Nakhodka

Wheat, rice, soybeans, sugar
beets, dairying, and stock
raising for beef

Wheat, soybeans, dairying, and
stock raising for beef

Forest industries with some
scattered agriculture along river
valleys

Tayga: reindeer herding,
hunting, trapping, and coastal
fishing

Suburban truck gardening

International boundary

Regional boundary

MILES

0   50   100   150   200   250

130°

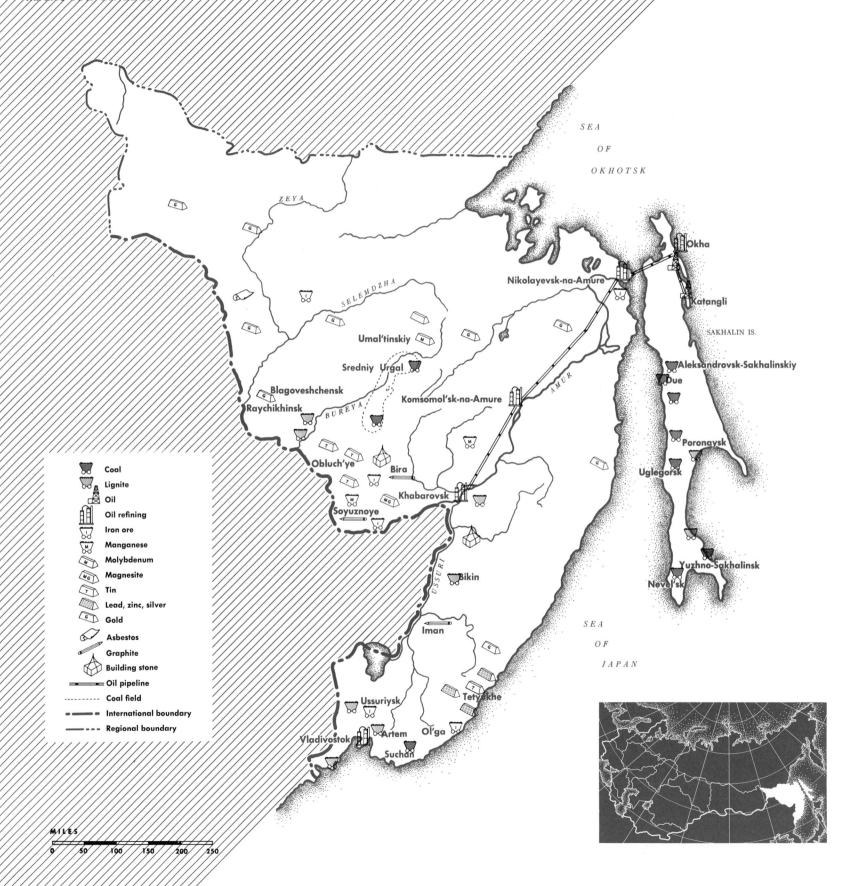

SEA
OF
OKHOTSK

ZEYA

Okha

SELEMDZHA

Nikolayevsk-na-Amure

Katangli

SAKHALIN IS.

Umal'tinskiy

Sredniy Urgal

Aleksandrovsk-Sakhalinskiy

Due

Blagoveshchensk

AMUR

Raychikhinsk

Komsomol'sk-na-Amure

BUREYA

Poronaysk

Uglegorsk

Obluch'ye

Bira

Khabarovsk

Soyuznoye

Yuzhno-Sakhalinsk

Nevel'sk

USSURI

Bikin

SEA
OF
JAPAN

Iman

Tetyukhe

Ussuriysk

Ol'ga

Vladivostok

Artem

Suchan

Legend

	Coal
	Lignite
	Oil
	Oil refining
	Iron ore
	Manganese
	Molybdenum
	Magnesite
	Tin
	Lead, zinc, silver
	Gold
	Asbestos
	Graphite
	Building stone
	Oil pipeline
	Coal field
	International boundary
	Regional boundary

MILES

0   50   100   150   200   250

130°

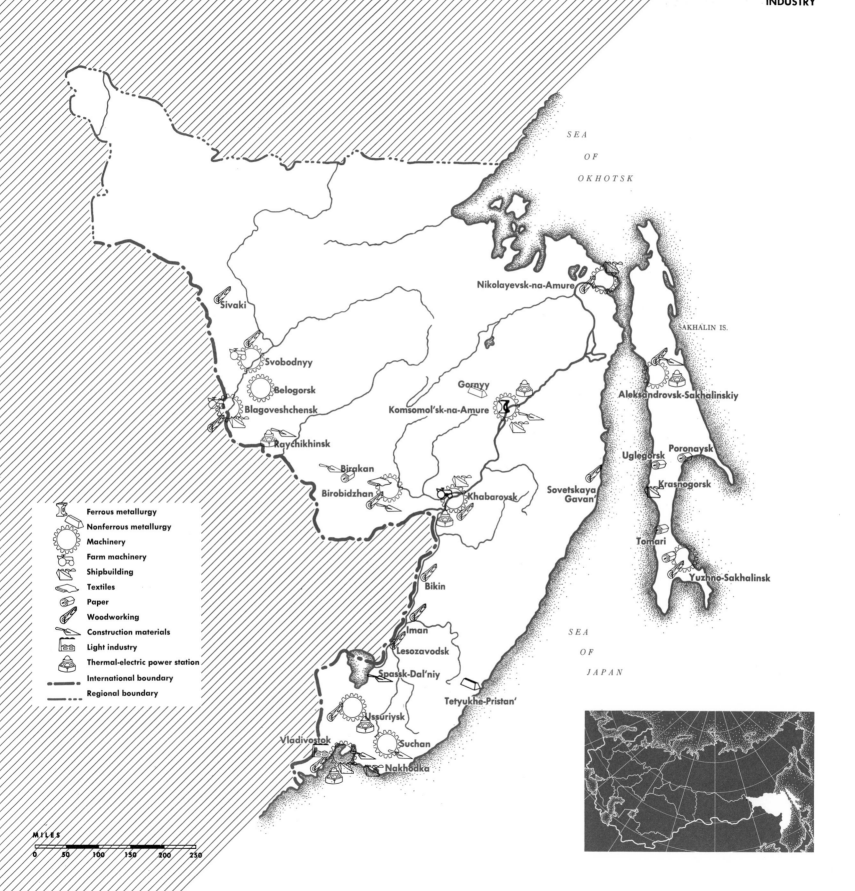

SEA
OF
OKHOTSK

SAKHALIN IS.

Sivaki

Nikolayevsk-na-Amure

Svobodnyy

Belogorsk

Gornyy

Aleksandrovsk-Sakhalinskiy

Blagoveshchensk

Komsomol'sk-na-Amure

Raychikhinsk

Poronaysk

Birakan

Uglegorsk

Krasnogorsk

Birobidzhan

Sovetskaya
Gavan'

Khabarovsk

Tomari

Yuzhno-Sakhalinsk

Bikin

SEA
OF
JAPAN

Iman

Lesozavodsk

Spassk-Dal'niy

Tetyukhe-Pristan'

Ussuriysk

Vladivostok

Suchan

Nakhodka

Legend

- Ferrous metallurgy
- Nonferrous metallurgy
- Machinery
- Farm machinery
- Shipbuilding
- Textiles
- Paper
- Woodworking
- Construction materials
- Light industry
- Thermal-electric power station
- International boundary
- Regional boundary

MILES

0   50   100   150   200   250

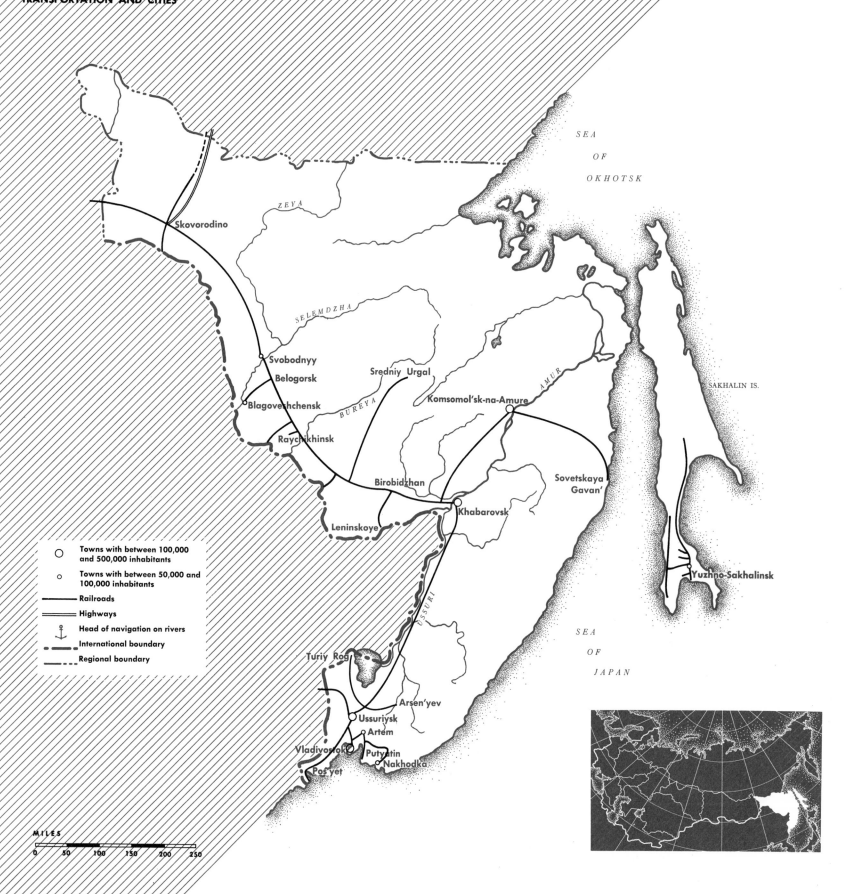

130°

SEA
OF
OKHOTSK

ZEYA

Skovorodino

SELEMDZHA

50°

Svobodnyy

Belogorsk

Sredniy Urgal

BUREYA

Komsomol'sk-na-Amure

AMUR

SAKHALIN IS.

Blagoveshchensk

Raychikhinsk

Birobidzhan

Sovetskaya
Gavan'

Leninskoye

Khabarovsk

Yuzhno-Sakhalinsk

USSURI

SEA
OF
JAPAN

Turiy Rog

Arsen'yev

Ussuriysk

Artem

Vladivostok   Putyatin
Pos'yet   Nakhodka

MILES

0   50   100   150   200   250

Legend:
○ Towns with between 100,000 and 500,000 inhabitants
○ Towns with between 50,000 and 100,000 inhabitants
— Railroads
= Highways
⚓ Head of navigation on rivers
—··— International boundary
—·— Regional boundary

130°

North Siberian and Northeastern Region

The North Siberian and Northeastern Region occupies close to one half of Soviet territory. It is the largest region, but the least populated, the least known, and the least developed. It extends nearly 4,000 miles from the eastern Urals to Bering Strait, and between 1,000 and 1,500 miles from the Arctic Ocean to the more densely inhabited regions of Western and Eastern Siberia and the Far East.

From the Urals to the Yenisey River North Siberia is flat and marshy. Between the Yenisey and the Lena rivers lies the low plateau of Central Siberia. Eastward from the Lena to Bering Strait and the Pacific the land is mountainous except for small coastal and river plains. In the far northeast the Kamchatka Peninsula extends southward into the Pacific, separating the Sea of Okhotsk from the open ocean.

The climate of the North Siberian–Northeastern Region is cold; the soils are everywhere underlain by permafrost, frozen subsoil. Farming is carried on in tiny clearings in the "tayga," the evergreen northern forest, and on experimental farms scattered throughout the region. Fishing offshore is limited, but the fur-bearing animals of the forest constitute a major industry. Furs brought the first Russian traders and trappers to Siberia, and furs of marten, mink, fox, sable, and ermine from the North Siberian "tayga" remain a major export of the Soviet Union.

Salt, mica, and gold have been mined in the southeastern part of this region for well over a century. Intensive prospecting since the early 1920s added a variety of other resources to those already known, among them tin, copper, graphite, nickel, lead, and zinc. The coal basin of the middle Lena Valley is believed to have the largest reserves of any coalfield in the country. In the late 1950s a major diamond field was discovered west of the Lena, and in the late 1960s new fields of oil and natural gas came gradually into production in the lower Ob' Basin, that may well become the most important Soviet sources of these vital fuels.

Transportation is one of the greatest problems the Soviet Union faces in developing the resources of this vast region. The Ob', Yenisey, and Lena are the three giant rivers of North Siberia; the Olenek, Yana, Indigirka, and Kolyma, although sizable streams, are dwarfed by comparison with the three giants. The short navigation season poses a major obstacle to their use, and shallow river beds, sand bars, and shifting courses further impede transportation. For bulk cargo and specialized goods, such as mining and construction machinery, the rivers are important in conjunction with the Great Northern Sea Route. Running from Murmansk and Arkhangel'sk in the west to Vladivostok in the east, the Great Northern Sea Route is an all-Soviet waterway and follows closely the Soviet shoreline in the Arctic and the Pacific. Its development has been largely carried out during the first half of the twentieth century, and it is now a permanent part of the Soviet system of ocean transport.

Besides trapping and mining, the North Siberian–Northeastern Region and the islands in the Soviet sector of the Arctic Ocean are important as centers of scientific research. A network of over one hundred polar stations carries out continuous observations of a variety of phenomena concerning climate, geophysics, and other matters.

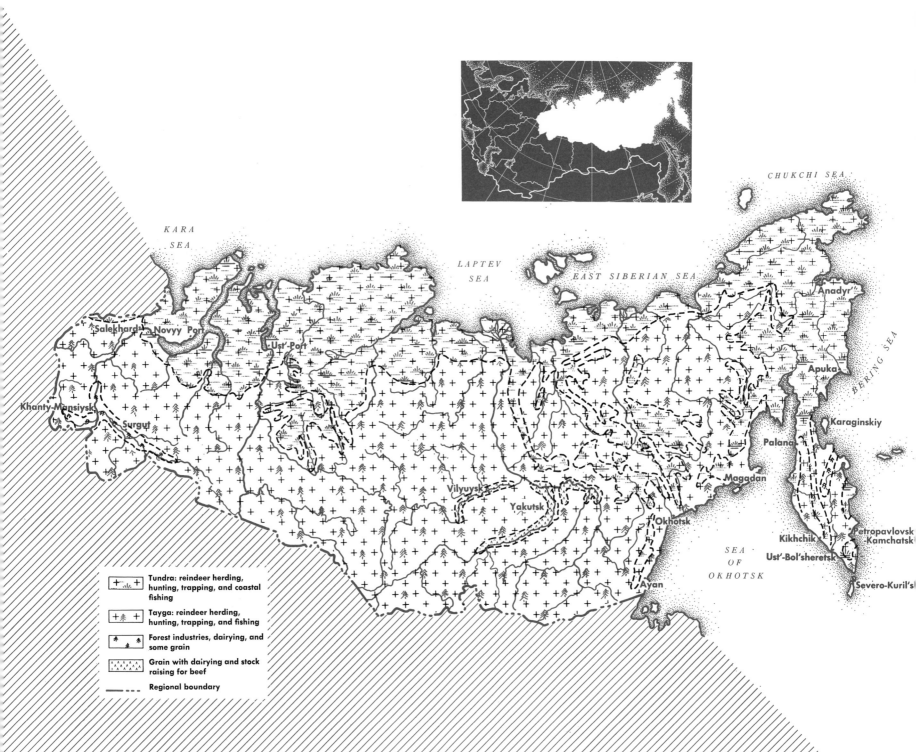

110°

KARA SEA

LAPTEV SEA

EAST SIBERIAN SEA

CHUKCHI SEA

BERING SEA

SEA OF OKHOTSK

Salekhard
Novyy Port
Ust'-Port
Khanty-Mansiysk
Surgut
Vilyuysk
Yakutsk
Okhotsk
Ayan
Magadan
Anadyr'
Apuka
Karaginskiy
Palana
Kikhchik
Ust'-Bol'sheretsk
Petropavlovsk-Kamchatsk
Severo-Kuril'sk

Tundra: reindeer herding, hunting, trapping, and coastal fishing	
Tayga: reindeer herding, hunting, trapping, and fishing	
Forest industries, dairying, and some grain	
Grain with dairying and stock raising for beef	
Regional boundary	

MILES

0   200   400   600

110°

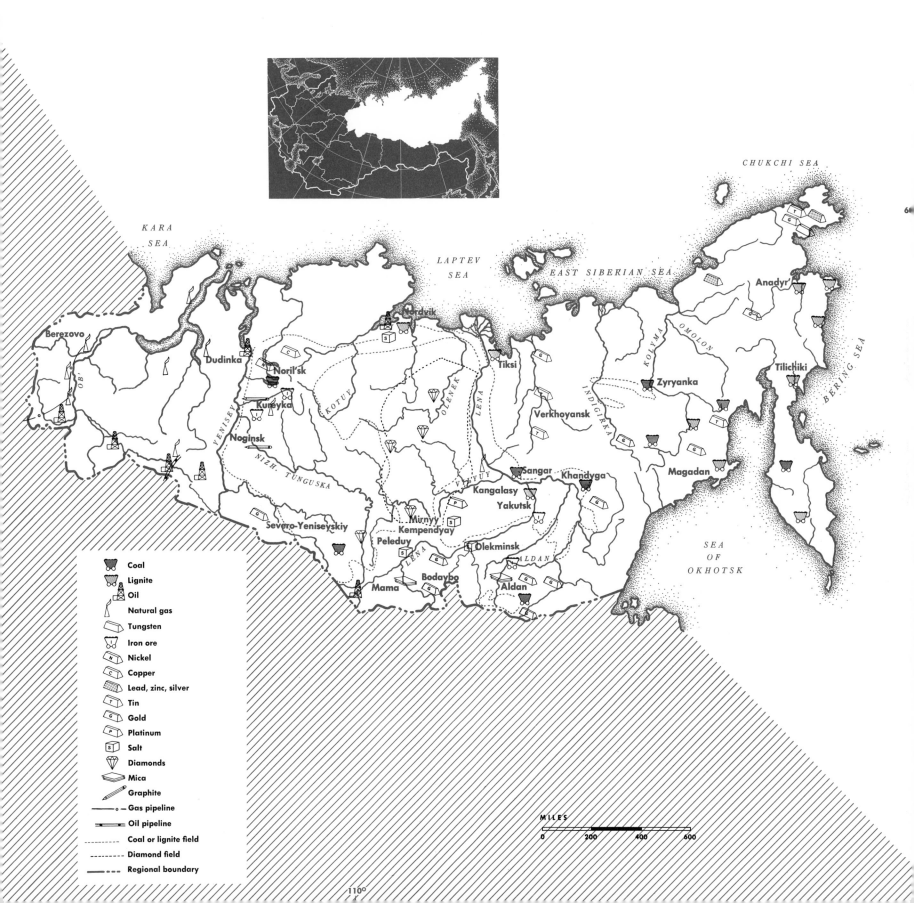

Legend

- Coal
- Lignite
- Oil
- Natural gas
- Tungsten
- Iron ore
- N Nickel
- C Copper
- Lead, zinc, silver
- T Tin
- G Gold
- P Platinum
- S Salt
- Diamonds
- Mica
- Graphite
- —o— Gas pipeline
- —■— Oil pipeline
- ---- Coal or lignite field
- ------ Diamond field
- —·—· Regional boundary

110°

CHUKCHI SEA

KARA SEA

LAPTEV SEA

EAST SIBERIAN SEA

BERING SEA

SEA OF OKHOTSK

Berezovo
Dudinka
Noril'sk
Kureyka
Noginsk
Severo-Yeniseyskiy
Nordvik
Tiksi
Anadyr'
Tilichiki
Zyryanka
Verkhoyansk
Magadan
Sangar
Khandyga
Kangalasy
Yakutsk
Mirnyy
Kempendyay
Peleduy
Mama
Bodaybo
Olekminsk
Aldan

OB'
YENISEY
NIZH. TUNGUSKA
KOTUY
OLENEK
LENA
VILYUY
ALDAN
KOLYMA
OMOLON
INDIGIRKA

MILES
0   200   400   600

110°

KARA SEA

LAPTEV SEA

EAST SIBERIAN SEA

CHUKCHI SEA

BERING SEA

SEA OF OKHOTSK

Salekhard

Noril'sk

Igarka

Khanty-Mansiysk

Bilibino

Magadan

Ust'-Kamchatsk

Klyuchi

Yakutsk

Petropavlo Kamchats

Kirensk

Peleduy

Bodaybo

Aldan

Nonferrous metallurgy

Ferrous metallurgy

Machinery

Shipbuilding

Woodworking

Construction materials

Light industry

Thermal-electric power station

Hydroelectric power station

Atomic power station

Regional boundary

MILES

0   200   400   600

110°

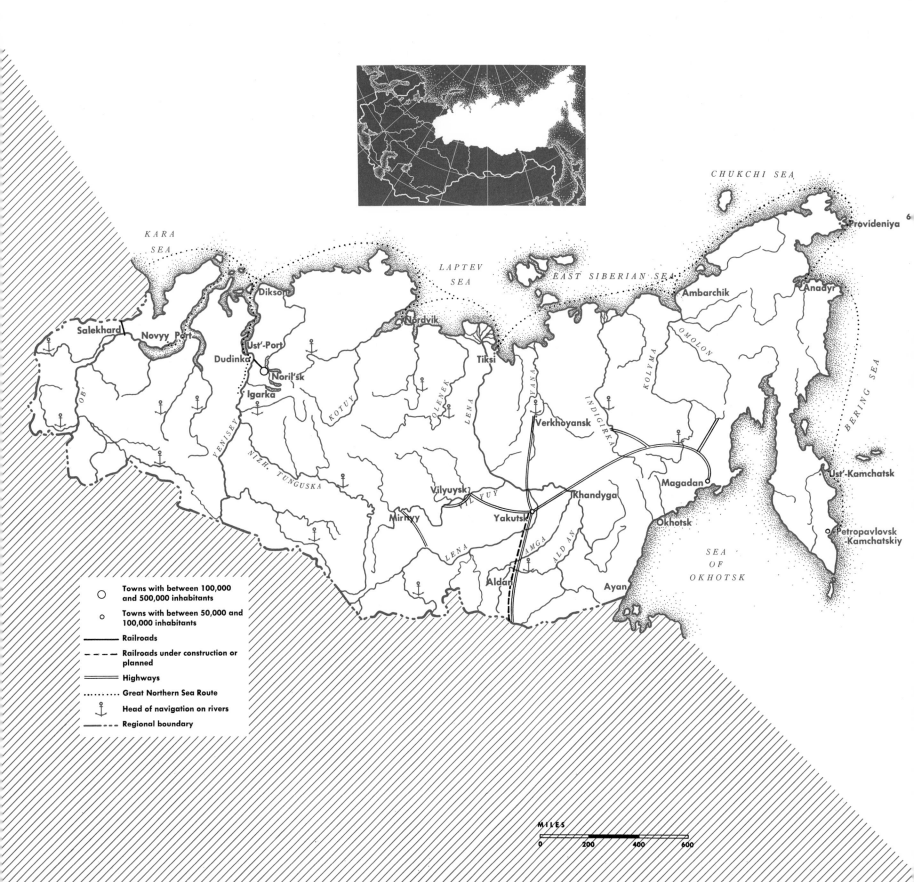

110°

CHUKCHI SEA

KARA SEA

LAPTEV SEA

EAST SIBERIAN SEA

Providieniya

Dikson

Ambarchik

Anadyr

Salekhard

Nordvik

Novyy Port

OMOLON

Ust'-Port

Tiksi

BERING SEA

Dudinka

Noril'sk

KOLYMA

Igarka

YENISEY

KOTUY

OLENEK

LENA

YANA

INDIGIRKA

Verkhoyansk

Ust'-Kamchatsk

NIZH. TUNGUSKA

Magadan

Vilyuysk

VILYUY

Khandyga

Mirnyy

Yakutsk

Okhotsk

Petropavlovsk Kamchatskiy

LENA

AMGA

ALDAN

Aldan

Ayan

SEA OF OKHOTSK

OB'

	Towns with between 100,000 and 500,000 inhabitants
O	
o	Towns with between 50,000 and 100,000 inhabitants
——	Railroads
- - -	Railroads under construction or planned
══	Highways
····	Great Northern Sea Route
⚓	Head of navigation on rivers
— - —	Regional boundary

MILES

0   200   400   600

110°

Southern Central Asia

Southern Central Asia is a region of striking contrasts in landscape, climate, settlement, and land use. The greater part of the region is desert, but in the foothills and valleys irrigation agriculture produces spectacular results. The almost completely dry climate of the interior plains, which stretch eastward from the Caspian, is contrasted with the substantial rainfall of the eastern, mountainous frontier. Most of the region is uninhabited, and the settlements are highly concentrated along railroads and in the fertile valleys.

The oases of Southern Central Asia trace their history back to the beginnings of agriculture in the first millennium B.C. The traditional contrast between settled farmers in the oases and wandering nomads on the desert fringe and in the mountains persisted until after the Russian conquest, which was completed in 1881. In recent years land under irrigation has been substantially enlarged, and Southern Central Asia is one of the Soviet Union's important regions of specialized agriculture. Cotton is the primary crop; millet, rice, and wheat are the cereals; and fruit of all kinds and silkworms are some of the special crops. Sheep and goats are raised in large numbers, and valuable pelts of sheep (kara-kul) are one of the leading products of the region.

Besides being the source of a variety of metals and minerals, including mirabilite (Glauber's salt), sulphur, and copper, the region produces coal and oil, and some hydroelectric power as well. In terms of the country as a whole, Southern Central Asia is most important as the leading producer of natural gas, transported by pipeline to the Urals and to the regions west of the Volga. The leading industries are smelting and refining, textiles, and food processing.

The administrative divisions of the region take into account the general distribution of the leading non-Russian peoples. Three of these belong to the Turkic group: the Uzbeks, Turkmens, and Kirgiz; the fourth group, the Tadzhiks, are related to the Persians. The administrative boundaries show an attempt to let each of the four republics share in the mountains, foothills, and valleys of the region. The peaks in the eastern part of the region, in the Kirgiz and Tadzhik republics, are the highest in the Soviet Union.

Tashkent, the largest city of Southern Central Asia, is the capital of the Uzbek Republic and the center of the region's railroad network. It is linked with Moscow, the Caspian Sea, and West Siberia. Among recently built railroads the line linking Tashkent with Dushanbe, capital of the Tadzhik Republic, and the line connecting the south shore of Lake Aral with the Tashkent–Caspian railroad are the most important.

Frunze, the capital of the Kirgiz Republic, and Ashkhabad, the capital of the Turkmen Republic, are their largest cities.

Very much in contrast with these and other relatively new cities, founded or substantially enlarged since the Russian conquest in the late nineteenth century, are the ancient oasis towns, Samarkand, Bukhara, and Khiva. Their history traces back to the days of Alexander the Great, and they have retained many monuments of former glory.

In contrast to Siberia, where the primitive aboriginals have either disappeared or retreated to remote areas, the natives of Central Asia, oasis dwellers and desert nomads, have long resisted Russian attempts at assimilation. Though the Soviet regime has completely changed the social, economic, and religious character of the region, the Central Asian peoples have retained to a large extent their distinctive dress and many of their old customs; they stand out in complete contrast to their Russian neighbors.

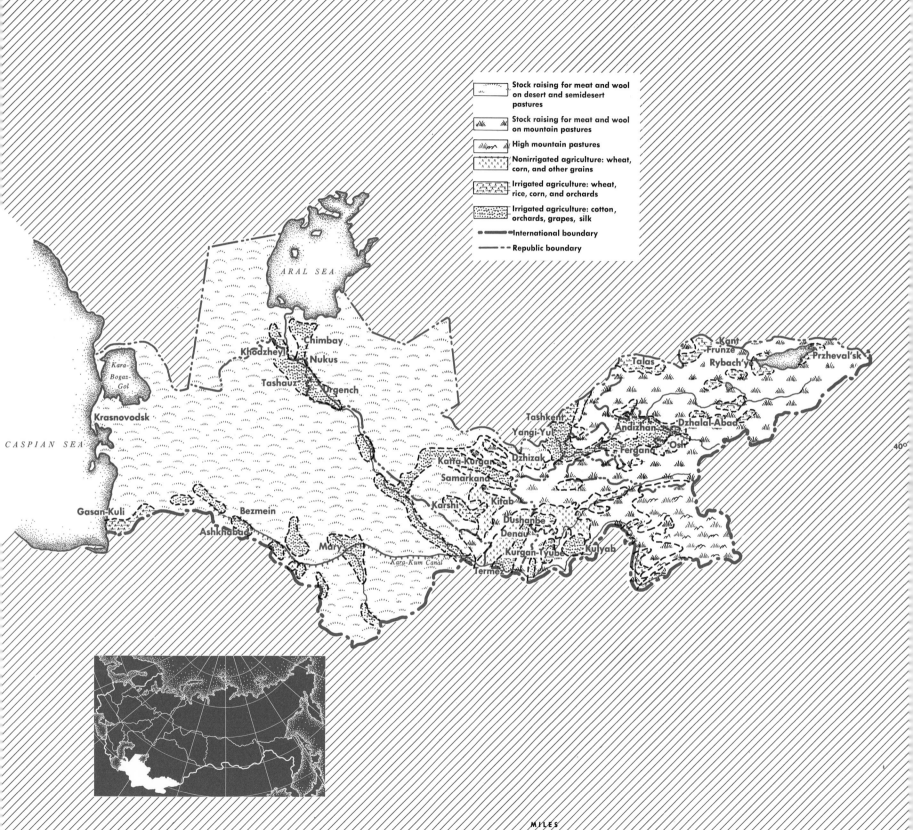

Stock raising for meat and wool on desert and semidesert pastures

Stock raising for meat and wool on mountain pastures

High mountain pastures

Nonirrigated agriculture: wheat, corn, and other grains

Irrigated agriculture: wheat, rice, corn, and orchards

Irrigated agriculture: cotton, orchards, grapes, silk

International boundary

Republic boundary

ARAL SEA

Chimbay
Khodzheyli
Nukus
Tashauz
Urgench

Kant
Frunze
Talas
Rybach'ye
Przheval'sk

Tashkent
Yangi-Yul
Andizhan
Dzhalal-Abad
Osh
Fergana

CASPIAN SEA

Kara-Bogaz-Gol

Krasnovodsk

Katta-Kurgan
Dzhizak
Samarkand
Karshi
Kitab

Gasan-Kuli
Bezmein
Ashkhabad
Mary
Dushanbe
Denau
Kurgan-Tyube
Kulyab

Kara-Kum Canal
Termez

40°

MILES
0   100   200   300   400

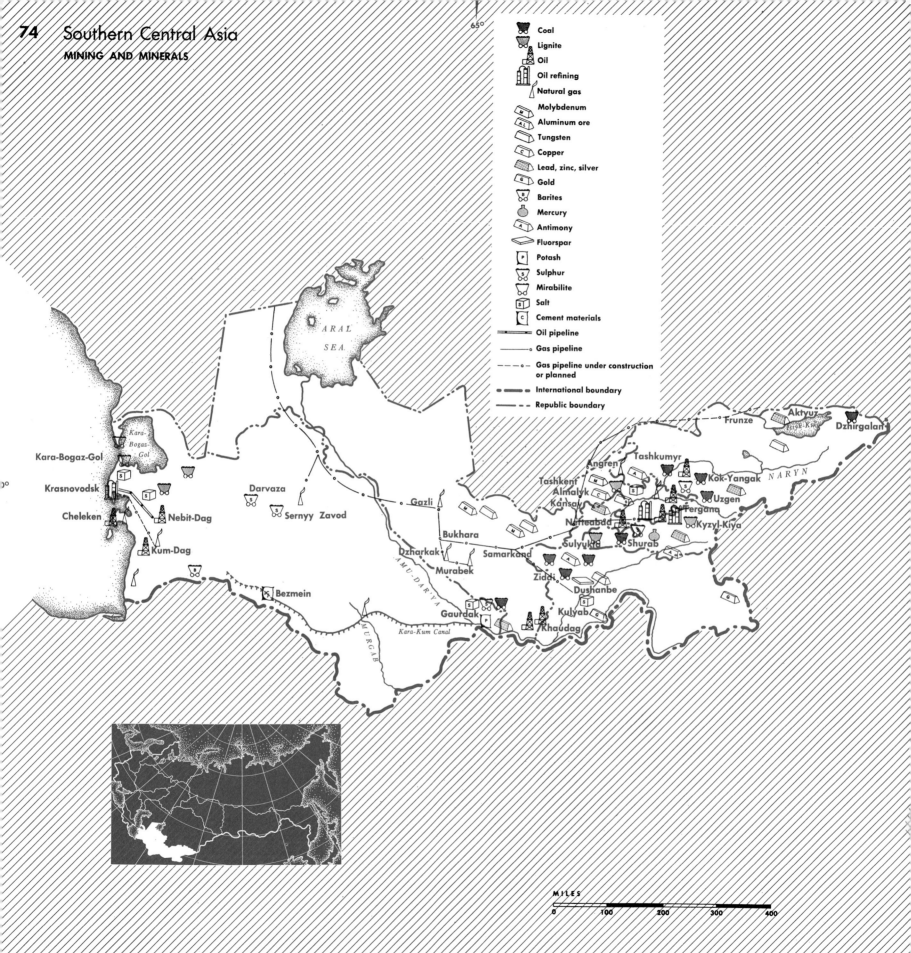

Coal
Lignite
Oil
Oil refining
Natural gas
Molybdenum
Aluminum ore
Tungsten
Copper
Lead, zinc, silver
Gold
Barites
Mercury
Antimony
Fluorspar
Potash
Sulphur
Mirabilite
Salt
Cement materials
Oil pipeline
Gas pipeline
Gas pipeline under construction or planned
International boundary
Republic boundary

ARAL SEA

Kara-Bogaz Gol

Kara-Bogaz-Gol

Krasnovodsk

Cheleken

Nebit-Dag

Kum-Dag

Darvaza

Sernyy Zavod

Gazli

Bukhara

Dzharkak

Murabek

Samarkand

Bezmein

AMU-DARYA

MURGAB

Kara-Kum Canal

Gaurdak

Khaudag

Ziddi

Dushanbe

Kulyab

Sulyukta

Shurab

Nefteabad

Kansai

Almalyk

Tashkent

Angren

Tashkumyr

Kok-Yangak

Uzgen

Fergana

Kyzyl-Kiya

NARYN

Frunze

Aktyuz

Dzhirgalan

MILES
0   100   200   300   400

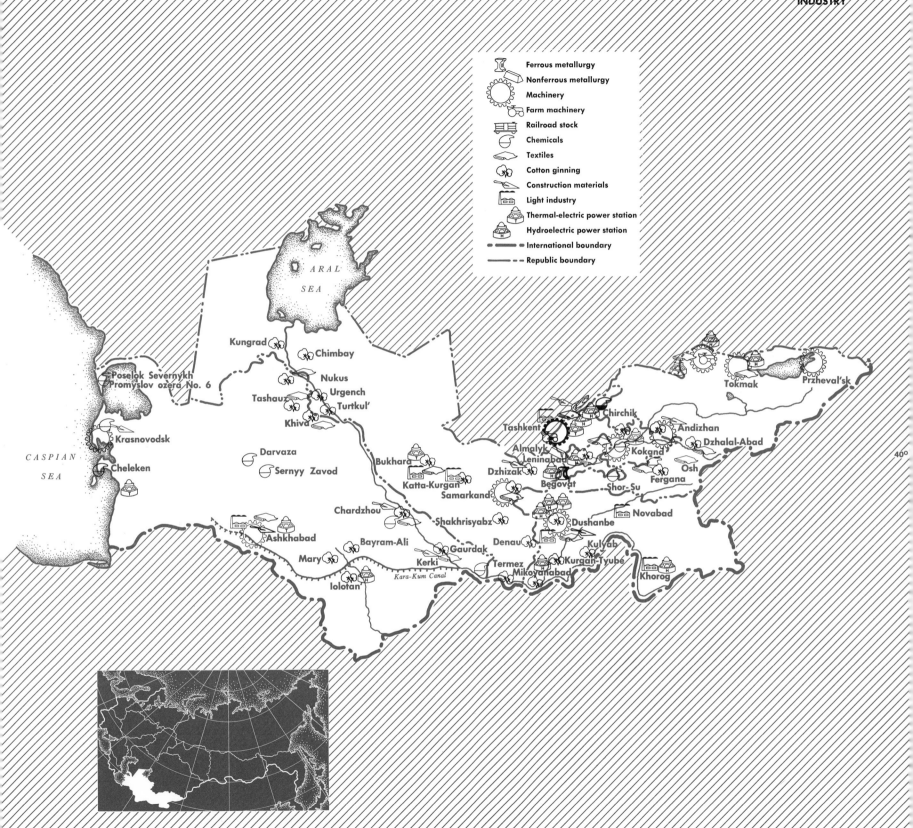

Ferrous metallurgy
Nonferrous metallurgy
Machinery
Farm machinery
Railroad stock
Chemicals
Textiles
Cotton ginning
Construction materials
Light industry
Thermal-electric power station
Hydroelectric power station
International boundary
Republic boundary

ARAL SEA

CASPIAN SEA

Kungrad
Chimbay
Nukus
Poselok Severnykh
Promyslov ozera No. 6
Tashauz
Urgench
Turtkul'
Khiva
Krasnovodsk
Darvaza
Sernyy Zavod
Bukhara
Cheleken
Katta-Kurgan
Samarkand
Chardzhou
Shakhrisyabz
Ashkhabad
Bayram-Ali
Gaurdak
Denau
Mary
Kerki
Kara-Kum Canal
Termez
Mikoyanabad
Iolotan

Tashkent
Chirchik
Almalyk
Leninabad
Dzhizak
Begovat
Dushanbe
Kokand
Shor-Su
Fergana
Osh
Andizhan
Dzhalal-Abad
Novabad
Kulyab
Kurgan-Tyube
Khorog
Tokmak
Przheval'sk

MILES
0   100   200   300   400

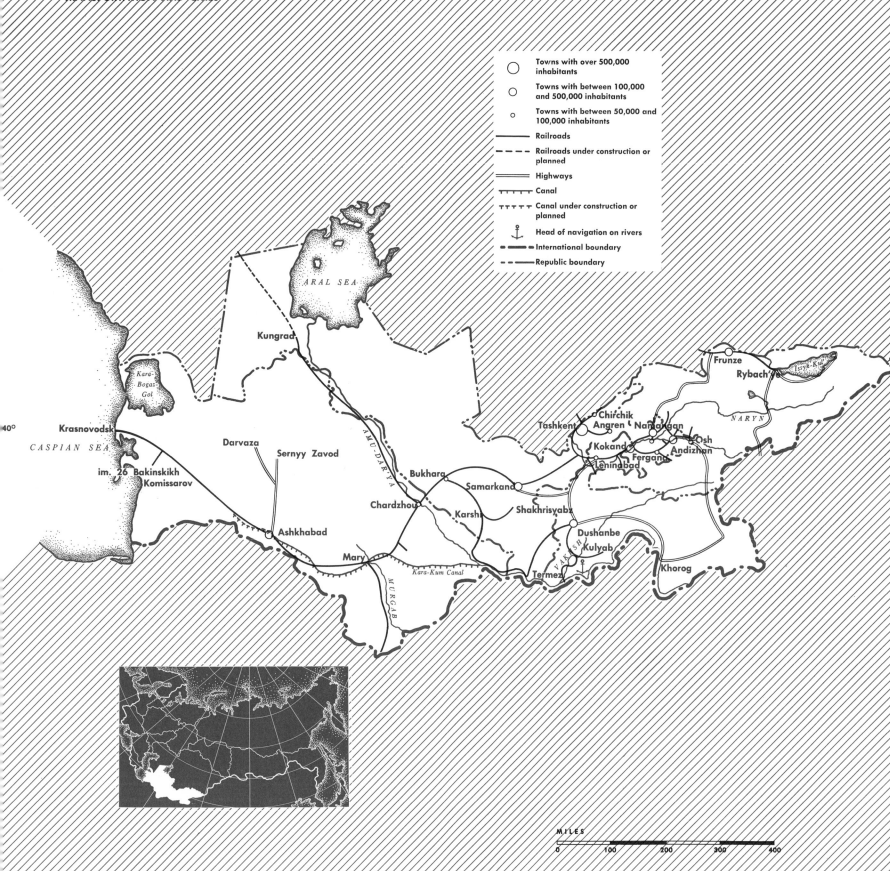

Towns with over 500,000 inhabitants

Towns with between 100,000 and 500,000 inhabitants

Towns with between 50,000 and 100,000 inhabitants

Railroads

Railroads under construction or planned

Highways

Canal

Canal under construction or planned

Head of navigation on rivers

International boundary

Republic boundary

65°

ARAL SEA

Kungrad

Kara-Bogaz-Gol

40°

Krasnovodsk

CASPIAN SEA

im. 26 Bakinskikh Komissarov

Darvaza

Sernyy Zavod

AMU-DARYA

Bukhara

Samarkand

Chardzhou

Karshi

Shakhrisyabz

Ashkhabad

Mary

MURGAB

Kara-Kum Canal

VAKSH

Termez

Dushanbe

Kulyab

Khorog

Frunze

Rybach'ye

Issyk-Kul

NARYN

Chirchik

Tashkent

Angren

Namangan

Kokand

Osh

Fergana

Andizhan

Leninabad

MILES

0   100   200   300   400

Kazakhstan—Northern Central Asia

Kazakhstan, the Kazakh Republic, is second largest in area of the constituent republics of the Soviet Union. It extends nearly two-thousand miles from the lower Volga in the west to the upper Irtysh River in the east, and almost a thousand miles from the limits of South Siberia in the north to its mountainous border in the south. The Kazakh Plateau occupies the core of the region—the lowlands to the north of the Caspian Sea, those surrounding Lake Aral, and those along the region's northern fringe—and the southern mountains make up the rest. Kazakhstan is a region of inland drainage; Syr-Dar'ya, Ili, Chu, and the other lesser rivers drain either to Lake Aral or to Lake Balkhash. Only the rivers of the northern and northeastern areas reach the Arctic Ocean. Most of the region is either desert or has limited and irregular rainfall, making farming hazardous at best.

Dry farming along the northern borders of Kazakhstan has been expanding at a considerable rate in the 1950s under the "virgin lands" scheme of bringing areas of marginal rainfall under cultivation. Wheat is the first crop, millet the second. Irrigation farming predominates in the valley of the Syr-Dar'ya and in the southern foothills and valleys. The orchards in the south are among the most productive in the Soviet Union. Stock raising has long been the main-stay of agriculture; sheep, goats, cattle, and pigs are pastured in the lowlands, and migratory husbandry is still practiced in the southern mountains.

The mineral resources of Kazakhstan are among the most important of the Soviet Union. Well over half of the country's copper, lead, zinc, nickel, chromium, and silver is mined in the Kazakh Plateau and in the heavily mineralized area in the easternmost part of the region. Coal is found in the Kazakh Plateau, at Karaganda, and Ekibastuz, and in the southern foothills near Chimkent. There is a producing oil field near the Caspian, the Emba field, and a major hydroelectric station operates on the upper Irtysh River.

Industrial establishments are widely scattered, located generally on the margins of the region, except the smelting and refining facilities at Karaganda and Balkhash. Aktyubinsk and Tselinograd in the north, Semipalatinsk and Ust'-Kamenogorsk in the northeast, and Chimkent in the south are the principal industrial centers. Alma-Ata, the capital of the Kazakh Republic, lies in the southern foothills.

The Russian conquest of this region took place during the nineteenth century, but the Kazakhs, the original inhabitants who had been nomadic herdsmen, were left undisturbed. Russian settlement was originally limited to the northern and southern fringes. The presence of valuable metals and minerals, the desire to expand crop acreage, and the necessity to establish good communications with European Russia and with the rest of Central Asia to the south led to the construction of railroads and a radical change in the pattern of settlement. Today more than half of the population of the region is Russian, and trunk railroad lines, built since the turn of the century, provide rapid mass transport to other parts of the country.

The Trans-Aral railroad, opened in 1907, connects the western part of Kazakhstan with Saratov, on the Volga, and Moscow. The Turk-Sib railroad, completed in 1930, links south and east Kazakhstan with West Siberia. The South Siberian railroad, completed after World War II, links the southern Urals with the Kuznetsk Basin of South Siberia, passing through northernmost Kazakhstan. From Tselinograd, a railroad, long in construction and completed in the 1950s, leads to the coal and copper mines of the Kazakh Plateau and the shores of Lake Balkhash and joins the Turk-Sib line south of this lake.

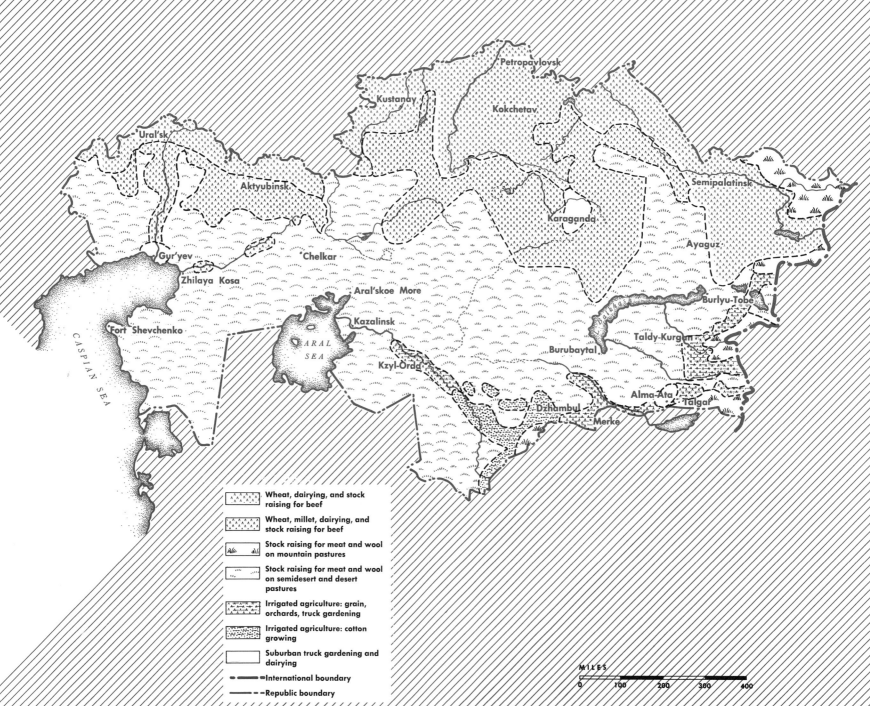

70°

50°

Petropavlovsk

Kustanay

Kokchetav

Ural'sk

Aktyubinsk

Semipalatinsk

Karaganda

Ayaguz

Gur'yev

Chelkar

Zhilaya Kosa

Aral'skoe More

Burlyu-Tobe

CASPIAN SEA

Fort Shevchenko

ARAL SEA

Kazalinsk

Taldy-Kurgan

Burubaytal

Kzyl-Orda

Balkhash

Alma-Ata

Talgar

Dzhambul

Merke

	Wheat, dairying, and stock raising for beef
	Wheat, millet, dairying, and stock raising for beef
	Stock raising for meat and wool on mountain pastures
	Stock raising for meat and wool on semidesert and desert pastures
	Irrigated agriculture: grain, orchards, truck gardening
	Irrigated agriculture: cotton growing
	Suburban truck gardening and dairying

International boundary

Republic boundary

MILES

0   100   200   300   400

70°

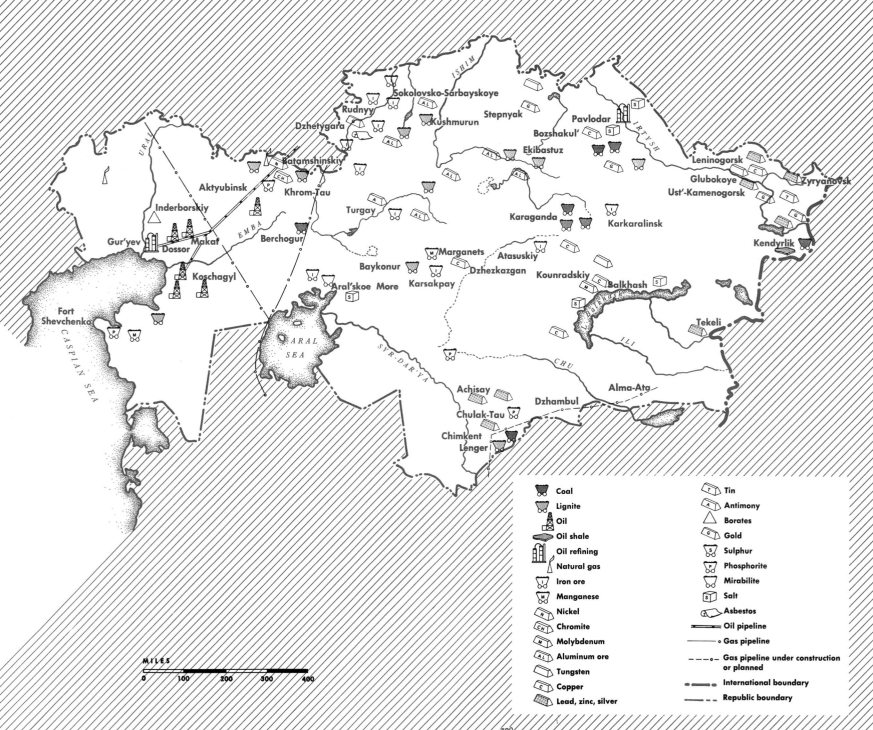

ISHIM

Sokolovsko-Sarbayskoye
Rudnyy
Dzhetygara
Stepnyak
Kushmurun
Pavlodar
Bozshakul'
Ekibastuz
Leninogorsk
Katamshinskiy
Glubokoye
Aktyubinsk
Ust'-Kamenogorsk
Zyryanovsk
Khrom-Tau
Inderborskiy
Turgay
Karaganda
Karkaralinsk
Gur'yev
Makat
Berchogur
Kendyrlik
Dossor
Marganets
Koschagyl
Baykonur
Atasuskiy
Dzhezkazgan
Kounradskiy
Balkhash
Aral'skoe More
Karsakpay
Fort
Shevchenka
Tekeli
CASPIAN SEA
ARAL SEA
SYR-DAR'YA
CHU
ILI
Achisay
Alma-Ata
Dzhambul
Chulak-Tau
Chimkent
Lenger

URAL
EMBA
IRTYSH

🛒	**Coal**	🔺 **Tin** (T)
🛒	**Lignite**	**Antimony** (A)
🛢	**Oil**	△ **Borates**
	Oil shale	**Gold** (G)
🏭	**Oil refining**	**Sulphur** (S)
	Natural gas	**Phosphorite** (P)
	Iron ore (I)	🛒 **Mirabilite**
	Manganese (M)	**Salt** (S)
	Nickel (N)	**Asbestos** (A)
	Chromite (CH)	**Oil pipeline**
	Molybdenum (M)	**Gas pipeline**
	Aluminum ore (AL)	**Gas pipeline under construction or planned**
	Tungsten (T)	**International boundary**
	Copper (C)	**Republic boundary**
	Lead, zinc, silver	

MILES
0   100   200   300   400

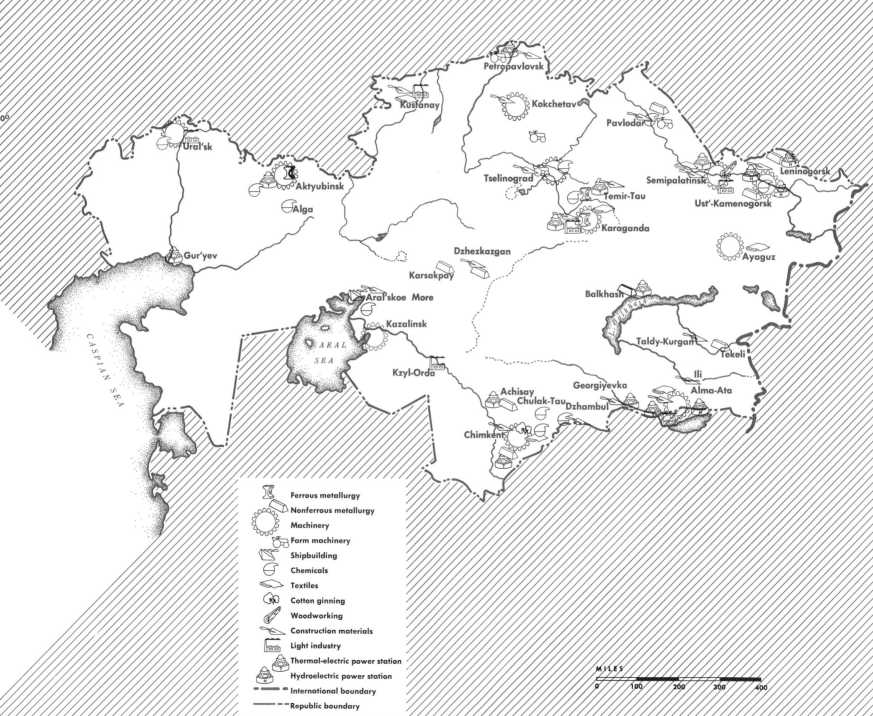

Petropavlovsk

Kustanay

Kokchetav

Pavlodar

Ural'sk

Semipalatinsk

Leninogorsk

Aktyubinsk

Tselinograd

Temir-Tau

Ust'-Kamenogorsk

Alga

Karaganda

Gur'yev

Dzhezkazgan

Ayaguz

Karsakpay

Balkhash

Aral'skoe More

Kazalinsk

Taldy-Kurgan

*ARAL
SEA*

Tekeli

Kzyl-Orda

Ili

CASPIAN SEA

Achisay
Chulak-Tau

Georgiyevka

Alma-Ata

Dzhambul

Chimkent

⚒	**Ferrous metallurgy**
	Nonferrous metallurgy
⚙	**Machinery**
	Farm machinery
	Shipbuilding
	Chemicals
	Textiles
	Cotton ginning
	Woodworking
	Construction materials
	Light industry
	Thermal-electric power station
	Hydroelectric power station
	International boundary
	Republic boundary

MILES

0   100   200   300   400

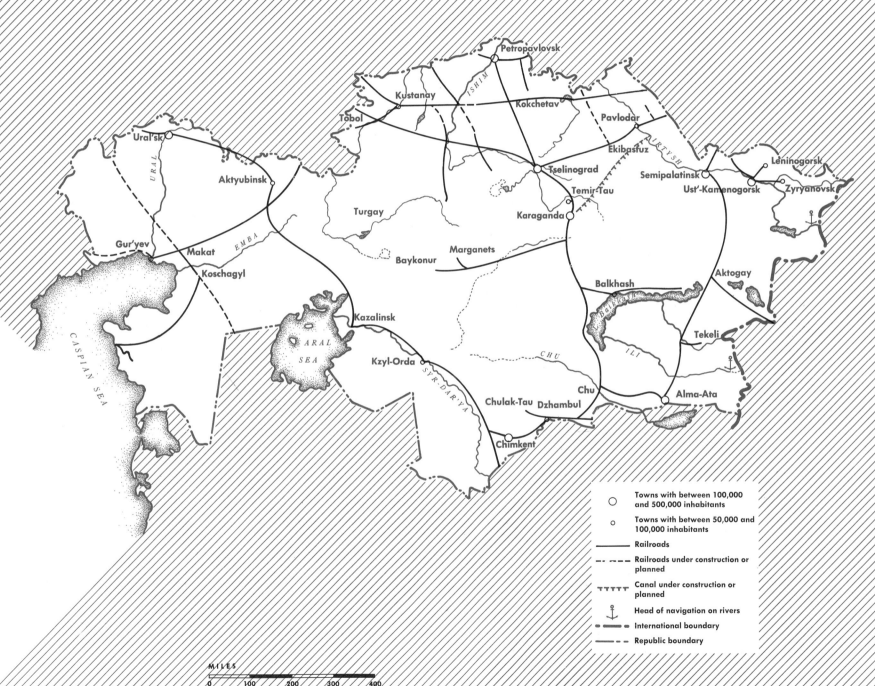

Petropavlovsk

Kustanay

ISHIM

Kokchetav

Pavlodar

Tobol

IRTYSH

Ural'sk

Ekibastuz

Leninogorsk

URAL

Tselinograd

Semipalatinsk

Aktyubinsk

Temir-Tau

Ust'-Kamenogorsk

Zyryanovsk

Turgay

Karaganda

EMBA

Gur'yev

Makat

Marganets

Koschagyl

Baykonur

Balkhash

Aktogay

BALKHASH

CASPIAN SEA

Kazalinsk

ARAL SEA

ILI

Tekeli

Kzyl-Orda

SYR-DAR'YA

CHU

Chu

Alma-Ata

Chulak-Tau

Dzhambul

Chimkent

Towns with between 100,000
and 500,000 inhabitants

Towns with between 50,000 and
100,000 inhabitants

Railroads

Railroads under construction or
planned

Canal under construction or
planned

Head of navigation on rivers

International boundary

Republic boundary

MILES

0   100   200   300   400

Bibliography

General

Atlas Mira. Moscow, 1959.

Baranskiy, N. N. *Economic Geography of the U.S.S.R.* Moscow, 1956.

Bol'shaya Sovetskaya Entsiklopediya, including *Yezhegodnik B.S.E.* Moscow, 1957 and 1958.

Bol'shoy Sovetskiy Atlas Mira. Vol. 2. Moscow, 1939.

Breyterman, A. D. *Ekonomicheskaya Geografiya S.S.S.R.* Part 1 (Geography of Heavy Industry). Leningrad University Press, 1958.

Cherdantsev, G. N., Nikitin, N. P., and Tutykhin, B. A. *Ekonomicheskaya Geografiya S.S.S.R.* General characteristics and geography of branches of the national economy of the U.S.S.R. Moscow, 1958.

———. *Ekonomicheskaya Geografiya S.S.S.R.* (R.S.F.S.R.) Moscow, 1956.

———. *Ekonomicheskaya Geografiya S.S.S.R.* (Ukrainian, Moldavian, Belorussian, Lithuanian, Latvian, Estonian, Georgian, Azerbaydzhan, Armenian, Kazakh, Uzbek, Kirgiz, Tadzhik, and Turkmen Republics.) Moscow, 1957.

Geograficheskiy Atlas. For teachers of Intermediate School. Second edition. Moscow, 1959.

Kostennikov, V. M. *Ekonomicheskiye Rayony S.S.S.R.* Moscow, 1958.

Lyalikov, N. I., Kabo, R. M., Davidov, E. M., and Voskresenskiy, S. S. *Geografiya S.S.S.R.* A textbook for teachers. Moscow, 1955.

Moscow News. Twice weekly. Moscow.

Ogonek. Monthly illustrated periodical. Moscow.

Sarantsev, P. L. *Geografiya Putey Soobshcheniya.* Moscow, 1958.

Soviet Union. Monthly illustrated periodical. Moscow.

Soviet Weekly. Moscow.

S.S.S.R. Administrativnoye-territorial'noye deleniye Soyuznykh Respublik. Moscow, 1958.

S.S.S.R. kak on yest'. Popular handbook. Moscow, 1959.

Ukazatel' zheleznodorozhnykh passazhirskikh soobshcheniy. Moscow, 1958.

Vedomosti Verkhovnogo Soveta. Moscow, 1958 and 1959.

Russian Soviet Federated Socialist Republic

Buyantuyev, B. R., Krotov, V. A., and Rozenfeld, Sh. L. *Problemy razvitiya promyshlennosti i transporta Buryatskoy A.S.S.R.* Moscow, 1958.

Cherdantsev, G. N., Nikitin, N. P., and Tutykhin, B. A. *Ekonomicheskaya Geografiya S.S.S.R.* (R.S.F.S.R.) Moscow, 1956.

Dolgopolov, K. V., Pokshishevskiy, V. V., and Ryazantsev, S. N. *Povolzh'ye.* Moscow, 1957.

Grigor'yev, A. A., and Ivanov, A. V. *Karel'skaya A.S.S.R.* Moscow, 1956.

Margolin, A. B. *Priamur'ye.* Moscow, 1957.

Maslev, E. P., Gozulov, A. I., and Ryazantsev, S. N. *Severnyy Kavkaz.* Moscow, 1957.

Mikhaylov, N. I. *Sibir'.* A physical geographical study. Moscow, 1956.

Pokshishevskiy, V. V. *Yakutiya.* Nature, people, and economy. Moscow, 1957.

Pomus, M. I. *Zapadnaya Sibir'*. Economic geographical characteristics. Moscow, 1956.

Skorodumova, I. P., and Semenov, L. V. *Krasnoyarskiy Kray*. Moscow, 1958.

Stepanov, A. A. *Khabarovskiy Kray*. Khabarovsk, 1957.

Stepanov, P. N. *Ural*. Moscow, 1957.

Tsunts, M. *Velikiye stroyki na rekakh Sibiri*. Moscow, 1956.

Udovenko, V. G. *Dal'niy Vostok*. Economic geographical characteristics. Moscow, 1957.

Vasyutin, V. F., Slavin, S. V., and Vilenskiy, M. A. *Problemy razvitiya promyshlennosti i transporta Yakutskoy A.S.S.R.* Moscow, 1958.

Zabelin, I. M., Al'bitskaya, K. A., and Rozental', R. E. *Rossiyskaya Sovetskaya Federativnaya Sotsialisticheskaya Respublika*. In series: Sovetskiy Soyuz. Kratkiye geograficheskiye spravki. Moscow, 1956.

Ukrainian and Moldavian Republics

Atlas sil'skoho hospodarstva Ukrainskoi R.S.R. Kiev, 1958.

Dobronravova, A. O., and Tugarinov, D. N. *Ukrainskaya S.S.R., Belorusskaya S.S.R., Moldavskaya S.S.R.* In series: Sovetskiy Soyuz. Kratkiye geograficheskiye spravki. Moscow, 1956.

Khizhnyak, A. A. *Nizhneye Pridneprov'ye*. Economic geographical study. Moscow, 1956.

Lyalikov, N. I. *Sovetskaya Ukraina*. Economic geographical study. Moscow, 1954.

Lymonnyk, A. *Ekonomichni administratyvni rayony Ukrainskoi R.S.R.* Kiev, 1957.

Nesterenko, A. A., Koroyed, A. S., and Gradov, G. L. *Ukrainskaya S.S.R.* Parts 1 and 2. Moscow, 1957.

Odud, A. L. *Moldavskaya S.S.R.* Moscow, 1955.

Belorussian and Baltic Republics

Belyukas, K. K., Bulavas, Yu. I., and Komar. I. V. *Litovskaya S.S.R.*

Bumber, Ya. F., and Alampiyev, P. M. *Latviyskaya S.S.R.* Economic geographical study. Riga, 1956.

Kovalevskiy, G. T., and Martinkevich, F. S. *Belorusskaya S.S.R.* Moscow, 1957.

Lill', V., and Maamyagi, V. *Estonskaya S.S.R.* Short historical-economic sketch. Moscow, 1955.

Rostovtsev, M. I., and Tarmisto, V. Yu. *Estonskaya S.S.R.* Economic geographical characteristics. Moscow, 1957.

Veys, E. E., and Purin, V. R. *Latviyskaya S.S.R.* Economic geographical characteristics. Moscow, 1957.

Armenian, Azerbaydzhan, and Georgian Republics

Al'bitskaya, K. A., Dobronravova, A. O., and Tugarinov, D. N. *Gruzinskaya S.S.R., Azerbaydzhanskaya S.S.R., Armyanskaya S.S.R.* In series: Sovetskiy Soyuz. Kratkiye geograficheskiye spravki. Moscow, 1956.

Dzavakhishvili, Al., and Shakarishvili, I. *Fizicheskaya geografiya Gruzinskoy S.S.R.* Textbook for the 7th class. Tbilisi, 1956.

Dzavakhishvili, A. N., and Ryazantsev, S. N. *Gruzinskaya S.S.R.* Economic geographical characteristics. Moscow, 1956.

Kashkay, M. A., and Alampiyev, P. M. *Azerbaydzhanskaya S.S.R.* Economic geographical characteristics. Moscow, 1957.

Marukhyan, A. D., Murzayev, E. M., and Ryazantsev, S. N. *Armyanskaya S.S.R.* Moscow, 1955.

Tavadze, F. N. *Prirodnyye resursy Gruzinskoy S.S.R.* Vol. 1. Metallic minerals. Vol. 2. Nonmetallic minerals. Moscow, 1958–59.

Kazakh and Central Asian Republics

Alampiyev, P. *Soviet Kazakhstan*. Moscow, 1958.

Al'bitskaya, K. A., Tugarinov, D. N., Zabelin, I. M., and Zakharova, T. K. *Kazakhskaya S.S.R., Uzbekskaya S.S.R., Kirgizskaya S.S.R., Tadzhikskaya S.S.R., Turkmenskaya S.S.R.* In series: Sovetskiy Soyuz. Kratkiye geograficheskiye spravki. Moscow, 1956.

Baranskiy, N. N. *Kazakhskaya S.S.R.* Economic geographical characteristics. Moscow, 1957.

Brover, I. M., and Yeroveyeva, N. A. *Promyshlennost' Kazakhstana za 40 let*. Alma-Ata, 1957.

Central Asian Review. London, S.W. 3, England: Central Asian Research Centre, 1953–59.

Chumichev, D. A. *Tadzhikskaya S.S.R.* Moscow, 1954.

Freykin, Z. G. *Turkmenskaya S.S.R.* Economic geographical characteristics. Second edition. Moscow, 1957.

Korzhenevskiy, N. L. *Uzbekskaya S.S.R.* Moscow, 1956.

Luknitskiy, P. *Soviet Tajikistan*. Moscow, 1954.

Narzikulov, I. K., and Ryazantsev, S. N. *Tadzhikskaya S.S.R.* Economic geographical characteristics. Moscow, 1956.

Pavlenko, V. F., and Ryazantsev, S. N. *Kirgizskaya S.S.R.* Moscow, 1956.

Pavlov, M. I. *Karakumskiy Kanal*. Moscow, 1955.

Vitkovich, V. *A Tour of Soviet Uzbekistan*. Moscow, 1954.

Zabelin, I. M. *Kazakhskaya S.S.R.* Moscow, 1958.

Index

(*Region in italic; boldface numerals refer to map groups*)